W9-CUQ-920

THE BRUINS

Also by Brian McFarlane

It Happened in Hockey

More It Happened in Hockey

Still More It Happened in Hockey

The Best of It Happened in Hockey

Stanley Cup Fever

Proud Past, Bright Future

It Happened in Baseball

The Leafs

The Habs

The Rangers

The Red Wings

THE BRUINS

BRIAN
MCFARLANE'S
ORIGINAL
SIX

BRIAN MCFARLANE

Stoddart

Copyright © 1999 by Brian McFarlane

All rights reserved. No part of this publication may be reproduced or
transmitted in any form or by any means, electronic or mechanical,
including photocopying, recording, or any information storage and retrieval
system, without permission in writing from the publisher.

Published in 1999 by Stoddart Publishing Co. Limited
34 Lesmill Road, Toronto, Canada M3B 2T6

Distributed in Canada by General Distribution Services Limited
325 Humber College Blvd., Toronto, Ontario M9W 7C3
Tel. (416) 213-1919   Fax (416) 213-1917
Email Customer.Service@ccmailgw.genpub.com

Distributed in the U.S. by General Distribution Services Inc.
85 River Rock Drive, Suite 202, Buffalo, New York 14207
Toll-free tel. 1-800-805-1083 Toll-free fax 1-800-481-6207
Email gdsinc@genpub.com

03 02 01 00 99   1 2 3 4 5

Cataloguing in Publication Data

McFarlane, Brian, 1931–
The Bruins

(Brian McFarlane's original six)

ISBN 0-7737-3189-X

1. Boston Bruins (Hockey team) – History.
I. Title.   II. Series: McFarlane, Brian, 1931–   .
Brian McFarlane's original six.

GV848.B68M33 1999   796.962'64'0974461   C99-931447-5

Every reasonable effort has been made to obtain reprint permissions.
The publisher will gladly receive any information that will help rectify,
in subsequent editions, any inadvertent omissions.

Jacket design: Bill Douglas @ The Bang
Jacket photo: Hockey Hall of Fame
Design and typesetting: Kinetics Design & Illustration

THE CANADA COUNCIL | LE CONSEIL DES ARTS
FOR THE ARTS | DU CANADA
SINCE 1957 | DEPUIS 1957

*We acknowledge for their financial support of our publishing program the
Canada Council, the Ontario Arts Council, and the Government of Canada
through the Book Publishing Industry Development Program (BPIDP).*

Printed and bound in Canada

To Bobby Orr,
who came as close to perfection on ice
as any NHL player I've ever seen

Contents

3

War-Time Hockey and Another Stanley Cup

4

Fireworks in the Fifties

5

Orr Comes to Town

6

The Big Bad Bruins

7

Bourque and O'Reilly Rule the Eighties

8

The Fascinating Nineties

Foreword

I am always amazed as I travel around North America to discover the widespread popularity of the Boston Bruins. They are without a doubt the most loved team of the Original Six clubs outside of Canada. Brian McFarlane has captured the spirit of the Bruins from the days of Shore to the days of Orr and beyond. The amazing stories Brian Kilrea tells of Eddie Shore in his coaching career are worth the price of this book alone. And I get the chance to tell a few of my favorite Shore yarns as well.

I found out for the first time, while reading this book, that I almost didn't get the Bruins' coaching job. That was a shocker.

I could go on about all this good stuff in the pages ahead, but I don't want to spoil it for you. This is one of those super books you won't want to put down until you've finished it.

Blue and I give it two thumbs and paws up!

Way to go, Brian!

Don Cherry
May 1999
Hockey Night in Canada *and the Mississauga Ice Dogs*

Acknowledgments

THE author wishes to thanks the many contributors to *The Bruins*, the fifth book in the Original Six series: Steve Dryden, editor-in-chief of *The Hockey News*, for permission to use excerpts from his excellent publication, including Bob McKenzie's article on Bobby Orr; Earl MacRae of the *Ottawa Sun* and Russ Conway of the St. Lawrence *Eagle-Tribune*; Eric Bulmash, Paul Patskou, Brian Beattie, Jonathon Rothman, and Norman Pawluck for their research and writing efforts; Don Cherry for his foreword; Brian Kilrea, Harry Sinden, Murray Henderson, Jerry Toppazzini, and Milt Schmidt; fact-checking wizard Ron Wight and editor Lloyd Davis; and Jim Gifford and Don Bastian, two fine editing specialists at Stoddart who've become my friends along the way.

1

Big-League Hockey Comes to Boston

Adams Brings Big-League Hockey to Boston

BORN in 1876, Charles Francis Adams, a poor boy from Newport, Vermont, never owned a hockey stick as a youth. But he was adept with a broom stick, working his way around the potato sacks, the feed bags, and the other merchandise in the corner grocery store where he first was employed as a chore boy. The proprietor, noting the meticulous attention young Adams gave to sweeping up dust and debris, said, "That lad shows a lot of promise. He'll probably be running his own store some day."

It was the start of a brilliant career in the grocery business, one that would propel Adams all the way to the chairmanship of First National Stores, one of the major chain store operations in the United States. The same unique, visionary qualities that made him hugely successful in business also served him well in the world of sport. A racing enthusiast, he was the founder, president, and owner of Suffolk Downs, and he was instrumental in getting parti-mutuel betting legalized in Massachusetts. In the mid-thirties, he was principal owner of the Boston Braves of the National League and used his powers of persuasion to get Sunday baseball approved in Boston.

"Where he got his interest in sports I don't know," his son Weston once said. "As a young man he worked so hard he had no time to play games himself."

When young Adams moved from Vermont to Brookline, Massachusetts, he discovered hockey and was hooked for life. He and Weston attended most of the club games played at the Boston Arena and in time he even sponsored a team, the Irish-Americans.

In 1924 Adams journeyed to Montreal to see the Stanley Cup finals and became even more enthused. "Those pros in the NHL can really play this game," he told his business associates. "I'm determined to get a team for Boston."

Weston would say, "When Dad got an idea in his head there was no stopping him. He gambled all his life on the things he believed in. And he had a strong belief in the future of hockey."

Adams applied for an NHL franchise at a meeting in Montreal on October 12, 1924, and was told that a man named Thomas Duggan had been granted two franchises on the condition they be placed in major U.S. cities. Adams snapped up one of the franchises for a fee of $15,000. Requests for franchises also came from Pittsburgh and Philadelphia, but these applications were shelved. Adams hired veteran hockey star Art Ross to run his team and to serve as governor. The Bruins played home games at the Boston Arena, which soon proved to be too small to house his new team. The Boston Garden, which opened in 1928, would not have been constructed if Adams had not guaranteed $500,000 rental for five seasons.

To acquire some manpower for his Bruins, Adams boldly peeled off $300,000 in 1926 to purchase an entire league in western Canada (more than forty players, including Eddie Shore).

Charles Adams enjoyed the thrill of three Stanley Cup championships. The first came the year the Garden opened, with the Bruins defeating the Rangers in a two-game final series.

A decade later, in 1939, the Bruins defeated Toronto for the Cup, and two years later they ousted Detroit in the finals.

Charles Adams was elected to the Hockey Hall of Fame in 1960 as a builder, indicating the high esteem in which he was held by his peers and associates in the game.

Montreal Woman
Names Bruins

EVER wonder how the Bruins got their name?

A young woman from Montreal gets most of the credit.

Bessie Moss, a transplanted Canadian, was secretary to Art Ross, formerly a renowned professional player and the first Boston general manager. In 1924, Charles F. Adams purchased the National Hockey League's first American franchise and selected Ross as the man most likely to bring hockey glory to Boston. Ross and Adams then faced the task of selecting a nickname and team colors for the new NHL entry. Miss Moss handled most of the correspondence between the two men pertaining to the subject.

The two men had no problem selecting the colors. Brown and gold were chosen because they emblazoned the storefronts of the grocery chain Adams owned. When Miss Moss learned that brown was one of the colors high on Adam's list she suggested the team be named the Bruins.

Adams and Ross liked the idea and tipped their hats to Miss Moss. While the brown in the original Boston uniform followed the selection of the Bruins as a nickname, many years later the club would drop the color brown and adopt gold, black, and white as the official team colors.

First Game at the Boston Garden

RESIDENT Charles F. Adams didn't want pregame formalities to hold up the opening of the new Boston Garden on the night of November 20, 1928. He didn't believe in long-winded speeches from politicians or time-wasting ceremonies on the ice. But he did want the Montreal Canadiens and their great star, Howie Morenz, to provide the opposition for the opener and the NHL was happy to oblige.

Adams announced that the doors to the new arena would open at seven o'clock, an hour and a half before the opening faceoff. The early opening would give fans a chance to wander through the corridors of the new building, marvel at its design, and to find their seats. He failed to anticipate that they would crowd against the gates in their zeal to be among the first inside, and would break windows and doors in a frenzy of excitement. Adams, when notified of the wild scene outside the building, ordered all doors to be thrown open immediately. His quick action prevented a disaster. Security guards were pushed aside by angry men intent on reaching the turnstiles. Women and children screamed, some ladies fainted, and dozens of extra policemen rushed to the scene.

Once inside the posh arena and safely in their seats, the paying customers, many of them dressed in evening attire, were entertained by the American Legion Band from Weymouth, Massachusetts. After the teams took their pregame warmup, 17,000 spectators, about 3,500 more than capacity, rose to sing the American and Canadian national anthems. Then the fans roared for more than five minutes, an explosion of sound that carried on well after the opening faceoff.

Meanwhile, outside the building, late arrivals continued to surge toward the building. Even as play began, people fought to hold their position in a line that stretched around the new North Station building and continued on down to the Warren Avenue Bridge. They sought the 1,500 seats Adams had advertised at fifty cents apiece and the additional 500 seats he'd put aside for one dollar per customer. Most fans were turned aside, bitterly disappointed.

The game itself produced only one goal, scored by Montreal's Sylvio Mantha. Mantha's hard shot struck goalie Tiny Thompson on the right pad and deflected into the corner of the net. Thompson, who had performed brilliantly in the minor leagues for Duluth and Minneapolis, was embarking on a career that would take him all the way to the Hockey Hall of Fame.

The opening-night loss, while disappointing, was one of only thirteen the Bruins would suffer that first season. They would get their revenge over the Canadiens in spectacular fashion four months later — in the playoffs for the Stanley Cup. In the opening round, Boston's Thompson collected a pair of shutouts as the Bruins ousted the Canadiens in three games. In the best-of-three finals against the Rangers, Thompson gave up but one goal as Boston swept to the Stanley Cup with two straight victories. The scores were 2–0 and 2–1. Tiny Thompson's playoff debut was spectacular — three shutouts in five games and a goals-against average of 0.60. The Bruins made their first season in the Boston Garden a memorable one, winning both the American Division championship and the Stanley Cup.

Shore's Arduous Journey

EDDIE Shore found himself caught in a Boston traffic jam on that January night in 1929. He was en route to the railroad station, where he would join his teammates and board the train for Montreal where there was a big game the following night. The traffic jam held Shore back by at least an hour. When he finally arrived at the station, the Bruins' train, with the team's special sleeper car bringing up the rear, was disappearing down the tracks. Shore sprinted after it, but to no avail.

Shore pondered his next move. He could drive to Canada, but it was a trip that would take all night. He decided his car was no match for the treacherous mountain roads of New England. So he phoned a wealthy friend, a longtime Bruins' fan, and asked if he could borrow a vehicle. The friend said he would not only send a powerful car over, he'd send his professional chauffeur along to drive it.

Eddie and the chauffeur left for Montreal immediately because the weather was threatening. A snowstorm was moving in. After a couple of hours on the road they ran into a blizzard. The chauffeur seemed uneasy at the wheel and had trouble keeping the car on the slippery road.

"Have you had any experience driving on snow and ice?" asked Shore. The man shook his head. Shore, who'd spent his youth shoveling out of the worst Saskatchewan snowstorms, said, "Well I have, let me take the wheel." The chauffeur readily agreed, switched places with Shore, and dropped off to sleep.

Shore wound up driving for the entire night. In the morning, he handed the wheel back to the chauffeur, ordered him to "drive safely and keep it under 20," and curled up in the back seat. He'd barely closed his eyes when he felt the car skid off of the road and roll into a ditch. Obviously, the chauffeur had panicked when the car slipped on a patch of ice. Eddie tumbled out of the back seat and went looking for help. Some distance down the road he found a garage but the manager told him there was no tow truck. "But I do have a hearse," the manager said. "Good," said Shore. "Gimme the keys. And let me borrow a chain." With the hearse and the chain, Shore was able to haul the borrowed car out of the ditch. Soon he and his shaken companion were once more en route to Montreal.

The two men arrived in Montreal late in the afternoon. Shore went straight to the Bruins' hotel and spotted two teammates, Cooney Weiland and Dit Clapper, sitting in the lobby. They were amazed to see him. "I'm going to hit the sack for an hour," he told them. "Wake me up when you're ready to go to the Forum."

Clapper and Weiland phoned Shore's room at six but got no answer. Shore slept through their call. The two Bruins hurried to Shore's room and doused him with a pitcher of cold water. That got him up in a hurry. At the Forum that night, Shore staggered out on the ice. "He won't be any good to us," one Bruin told another. "Look at the bags under his eyes. We could put our equipment in them."

But the roar of the hostile crowd was all the stimulation Shore needed. It was a wakeup call like no other. When he glanced down the ice and saw a swirl of opponents warming up, his pulses began to pound. These were the hated Maroons and he'd never sleepwalked through a game with them yet.

The story of the game was straight out of Hollywood. Shore pounded the Maroons with bodychecks that left many of them reeling. And when neither team could score, he took the offense and potted the only goal of the match. His arduous journey through the long wintry night had been worth it. His adventure had a very satisfying ending.

In the Boston dressing room after the game, Art Ross, the Bruins' manager, approached Shore as he rested his weary legs and stripped off his pads.

"Nice game, Eddie. I'm sure glad you made it here."

"Thanks, boss," said Shore. "It's a trip I'd like to forget."

"Then I've got something that'll remind you of it," Ross said, delivering the bad news. 'I'm fining you for missing the damn train in Boston."

Bruins Win Their
First Stanley Cup

WHEN the 1928–29 NHL season opened, the Boston Bruins presented a formidable lineup. They purchased Cy Denneny from Ottawa and named him player/coach. A new goaltender, Cecil "Tiny" Thompson, had moved in to replace aging Hal Winkler. Eddie Shore and Lionel Hitchman were at their peak on defense. Aubrey "Dit" Clapper and Norm "Dutch" Gainor were joined on a line by Ralph "Cooney" Weiland, called up from Minneapolis of the American Association. The trio would soon become known as the "Dynamite Line."

During the season, the Bruins introduced George Owen, a Harvard grad, to the Boston lineup, along with former Dartmouth star Myles Lane, acquired from the Rangers. The club traded Frank Frederickson to the Pittsburgh Pirates. Frederickson, in a display of class, wrote a letter of thanks to the Bruins for their treatment of him. The letter, published in a Boston paper, included the words, "I will always cherish the privilege of having the opportunity of knowing something about Boston and Bostonians."

The Bruins set an American Division record for most wins in a season (26) and scored the most goals (89). They finished two points behind the Canadiens in the overall standings and faced the Habs and their record-setting goaltender, George Hainsworth (22 shutouts in 44 games) in the first round of the playoffs. Hainsworth had allowed a mere 43 goals all season, less than one per game. Why the two top clubs met in the first round remains a mystery, one of the biggest bonehead decisions of that era.

While Hainsworth was brilliant in the first two games, Boston's Tiny Thompson was even better. He produced back-to-back 1–0 shutouts in Games One and Two, played in Boston. These stunning victories were followed by a 3–2 Bruins win at the Montreal

Forum in which Eddie Shore scored the winning goal. The Bruins were led by captain Lionel Hitchman, who played throughout Game Three with blood flowing from a huge gash in his head. At the final buzzer, Howie Morenz was the first Montreal player to race over and congratulate the Bruins.

When the train carrying the winners arrived back in Boston, the team was accorded the greatest reception for a Boston team in history. And the Stanley Cup was still a winning series away!

For the first time in the annals of the NHL, two American teams, the Bruins and the Rangers, met in the best-of-three final series for the Stanley Cup. Boston captured the first game on home ice, 2–0, behind Thompson's superb goaltending. It was his third shutout of the playoffs. Two nights later, at Madison Square Garden, Dr. Bill Carson of the Bruins scored with less than two minutes to play in regulation time to give the Bruins a 2–1 victory and the Stanley Cup.

Rookie netminder Tiny Thompson had played in all five games, recorded three shutouts, and given up a mere three goals. His goals-against average for the playoffs was 0.60.

Another wild celebration greeted the Bruins on their return to Boston and a few days later, at a gala affair in the Swiss Room of the Copley Plaza, the players gathered for a victory party. President Adams divvied up $35,000 in bonus money while the players surprised Adams with an unusual present — a two-foot-high bronze bear imported from Russia. Manager Art Ross received a set of golf clubs. Ross expressed his appreciation for the loyalty his players had displayed all season. "There has never been a professional team," he said, "where there has been less bickering, fewer jealousies, and better spirit. All season long that has been the case." He paid special tribute to Lionel Hitchman, an original Bruin, calling him "a cornerstone of the franchise."

Ross also remembered ex-goalie Hal Winkler, his name to be inscribed on the Stanley Cup even though Winkler's NHL career ended the season before.

Bruins Top the List

IT'S right there in the NHL's *Official Guide and Record Book.* The team with the best winning percentage for one season: Boston Bruins, 1929–30.

The Montreal Canadiens have won five straight Stanley Cups, the Detroit Red Wings have won 62 games in a season, the Edmonton Oilers have scored a record 446 goals, the Philadelphia Flyers once went undefeated for 35 games, but none of these powerhouse teams matched the record winning percentage of the '29–30 Bruins.

In only their sixth NHL season, the Bruins won 38 of 44 games, lost only 5, and tied one for a winning percentage of .875. That season the Bruins ran up two marvelous streaks, winning fourteen consecutive games and, later, another twelve straight games. They scored more goals (179) and gave up fewer (98) than any other club, and ace scorer Cooney Weiland won the scoring title with 43 goals and a record 73 points — a mark that lasted 14 seasons, until 1943–44, when Herb Cain, another Bruin, came along and scored 82 points.

The Bruins of 1929–30 had a superb roster of players. Seven were future Hall of Famers: goalie Tiny Thompson, defenseman Eddie Shore, and forwards Cooney Weiland, Mickey MacKay, Dit Clapper, Marty Barry, and Harry Oliver. Why then is this club not better remembered? Likely because they failed to win the Stanley Cup that season.

In the playoffs, after eliminating the Montreal Maroons, the Bruins ran into the red-hot goaltending of the Canadiens' George Hainsworth and were ousted in two straight games (3–0 and 4–3) in the best-of-three final. The Bruins had won 17 more games than the Habs and accumulated 26 more points. If the series had been best of seven, or even best of five, the outcome might have been different. But in the finals, in 120 minutes, it was all over for the team with the NHL's best winning percentage.

Cleghorn a Tough SOB

WHEN Sprague Cleghorn joined the Boston Bruins for the 1925–26 season he was 35 years old and his unsmiling face bore the scars of many hockey battles. Old Sprague took the game seriously and he treated every opposing player as he would a cockroach — as something to be squashed. "I figure I been in about fifty stretcher-case fights in my time," Cleghorn confessed. He recalled disabling three opponents in one game during a bloody match in Ottawa one night. He stated, with no trace of remorse, that he'd used his stick like a scalpel on Newsy Lalonde one night in Toronto, attempting to detach his scalp from the rest of his battered head. "They arrested me and charged me with assault," he recalled. "But my friend Newsy came to my aid, pleaded with the judge for leniency, and I got off with a $200 fine."

Newsy was a *friend*?

What about the time you had your leg in a cast and your wife charged you with hitting her with your crutch, Sprague?

"A minor domestic dispute. And frankly, none of your damn business."

Red Dutton, who had many confrontations with Cleghorn before retiring to become NHL president, shuddered at the memory of those run-ins. "He'd shave you right to the skull," said Dutton. "A mean man. Jesus, he was mean. And you never wanted to fall down in front of him because he'd try to kick your balls off."

Ottawa star King Clancy got cute with Cleghorn one night, rapping his stick on the ice and calling for a drop pass as he followed Sprague up the ice on a rush. Sprague dropped the pass and turned beet red when he turned and saw Clancy racing away in the opposite direction.

"I'll get even with that little pipsqueak," Cleghorn vowed.

At the end of the period, the teams headed for their dressing rooms. In the dark corridor, Clancy heard someone call out, "Hey,

King!" Clancy looked back and took a punch on the jaw that knocked him bowlegged. His assailant was Cleghorn. "That's for making me look bad," growled Cleghorn.

In 1923, Clancy's Ottawa Senators were engaged in a violent playoff battle with Cleghorn's Canadiens. Cleghorn took aim at Lionel Hitchman (who would later become a legendary Bruin) and laid him out with a vicious cross-check. While this was happening, Sprague's teammate Billy Coutu (sometimes called Couture) was busy smashing Cy Denneny over the head with his hockey stick, knocking him senseless. Leo Dandurand, the Montreal manager and a true sportsman, was so appalled he suspended his two headhunters and refused to let them play in the next game.

In time, Cleghorn, Coutu, and Hitchman would be lured to Boston by Art Ross. Ross enjoyed watching masters of mayhem like Cleghorn and Coutu go about their business. As an aging Bruin, Cleghorn's act didn't change, while Coutu would be suspended for life for striking an official after a game.

Hooley Smith, a hotshot 20-year-old with Ottawa when Cleghorn joined the Bruins, just shrugged when Clancy told him to beware of Cleghorn — on or off the ice. "Oh, he's not so tough," scoffed Smith. "And he's getting old and slow."

Smith gave Cleghorn a rough ride whenever they met, handing out some stiff checks that left the veteran fuming. But Sprague didn't retaliate — not right away.

Clancy picks up the rest of the story. "Hooley and I went for a meal after a game in Boston, a game in which Smith gave Cleghorn lots of grief. Suddenly Cleghorn and three or four Bruins appeared in the doorway of the restaurant and Cleghorn shouted a few words across the room at Smith. What he said was not very complimentary.

"Smith reached for a large ketchup bottle to use as a weapon. He said to me, 'King, this looks bad. Run outside and call a cop.'

"I ran past Cleghorn and his mates, pushing them aside, and raced outside. There were no cops to be found anywhere. My hotel was just a block away so I ran to get some of the Ottawa boys to form a rescue party. I hoped Smith would still be alive by the time we got back. But before I could round them up, Smith showed up — out of breath and still holding the ketchup bottle.

"'I swung that bottle in all directions and made my escape,' he told us. 'And a good thing I did because Cleghorn would have killed me if he'd got his hands on me. King, you were right about him. He's one tough sonofabitch — on and off the ice.'"

Cleghorn played three seasons on defense for the Bruins, from 1925–26 to 1927–28, and at age 37, the fires still burning, took a career-high number of penalties in his second-last season.

Shore's Sharp Skates

LIKE most perfectionists, Eddie Shore was not an easy man to get along with — on or off the ice. And when he felt there was something wrong with his skates or his sticks, he was quick to vent his wrath.

One night before a game at the Garden, Eddie put his nose in the face of Win Green, the Bruins' trainer. "Win, look at these bleeping blades! They're dull as hell. Get 'em sharpened, I can't play on these."

Shore's griping was old hat to Green. He took the skates, looked at his assistant Walter Randall, winked, and said, "Randall, go get 'em sharpened for Eddie." Much to the chagrin of Green and all the Bruins, the club had never purchased a skate sharpening machine. All of the sharpening was done at the Boston Arena, some distance away.

With Shore's precious skates under his arm, Randall flew out of the room, trotted down the ramp into North Station, and calmly took a seat in the railroad waiting room. He pulled out a newspaper and read the sports pages. Every few minutes he checked his watch.

When twenty minutes had passed, he turned to the Bruin dressing room and handed Shore his skates. Shore held the blades up to his eye and said with an approving smile, "Now, that's much better, Walter. That's how my skates should be sharpened all the time."

Shore played his usual spectacular game that night on blades that served him well. Randall saved himself a trip to the Boston Arena and the club saved itself a twenty-five cent sharpening fee.

Art Ross a Bruin Legend

ARTHUR Howie Ross is regarded as the man who established pro hockey in Boston and the man responsible for acquiring and developing many of the Bruins' greatest stars, including Woody Dumart, Bobby Bauer, Bill Cowley, Tiny Thompson, and Frank Brimsek.

Born in Naughton, Ontario, on January 13, 1886, Ross was many things to the game of hockey — a pioneer player, innovator, strategist, promoter, coach, manager, and official.

In his fourteen-year playing career as a defenseman, Ross played on two Stanley Cup championship teams — one in 1907 with Kenora (representing the smallest community ever to win the Cup) and another the following season with the Montreal Wanderers. His playing career ended in 1918 when he turned to refereeing.

From a manager's role with the Hamilton Tigers, he became manager-coach of the Boston Bruins when they joined the NHL in 1924. Later he would be promoted to general manager, vice president, and governor of the Bruins. He coached Boston on four separate occasions and Boston teams won three Stanley Cups under his direction — in 1928–29, 1938–39, and 1940–41.

As an innovator, Art Ross had few peers in the sport. The nets in use today in the NHL and in leagues around the world were designed by Ross. He improved the design of the hockey puck, adding beveled edges to it, and he devised the early helmets worn by NHL players. He was also responsible for many progressive rule changes in the game and he was the first coach to pull his goalie during a playoff game.

One rule he insisted on during his stint as Boston manager baffled many of his players. A defenseman who took a shot on goal during a game would be fined. Eddie Shore was not a fan of the Ross strategy. "Art wanted his defensemen to throw the puck to a forward at all times because the forwards were supposed to be better shooters."

Somewhere along the way, Ross rescinded his rule. A good thing, too, because Shore alone scored 103 goals during his career.

The Ross name is still in the NHL record book. He's the only coach to have compiled an .875 winning percentage, the highest in NHL history. In 1929–30, his Bruins went 38–5–1. The Montreal Canadiens spoiled this incredible season by winning the Stanley Cup in a best-of-three final series, 3–0 and 4–3.

Ross was inducted into the Hockey Hall of Fame in 1945. The trophy awarded to the NHL scoring champion each year bears his name. He died in Boston in 1964.

Dit Was Durable

I F you ever wonder why oldtime Bruin Aubrey "Dit" Clapper is in the Hockey Hall of Fame, listen to this. The guy played in the NHL for twenty years — the first player in history to perform for two full decades. He's the only NHL player to be listed on the NHL All-Star Team at both forward and defense (even Red Kelly couldn't match that feat), and he remains the only Bruin to play on three Stanley Cup–winning teams.

Clapper broke in with the Bruins as a strapping right winger in 1927–28. The following year he found himself sipping bubbly from the Stanley Cup. He played on the dangerous Dynamite

Line with Cooney Weiland and Dutch Gainor, and in his third season, 1929–30, he exploded for 41 goals in 44 games, helping the Bruins to an almost-perfect 38–5–1 record. Postseason glory eluded Clapper and the Bruins as they fell to the Montreal Canadiens in an uncommon two-game final series, 3–0 and 4–3.

By 1937, told he'd lost a step as a forward, he shrugged and moved back to defense. Within a year he was so proficient in his new role that he made the First All-Star Team. Despite his size and strength he was known as a clean, sportsmanlike player. And he earned plenty of respect. One night after an altercation on the ice he lashed out and punched the referee, a young chap named Clarence Campbell. Campbell was so astonished at this uncharacteristic outburst that he recommended leniency. Campbell confessed that he had provoked the Bruin star. "I called Clapper a name that angered him. I was wrong to do so." The result was a one-game suspension.

Prior to the 1945–46 season Clapper was named player-coach of the Bruins and guided them to the '46 finals. In February of the following year he bowed out as a player. But coaching didn't provide any greater satisfaction. "I found it difficult coaching players who were my longtime friends," he said. He resigned after the 1948–49 season. The Bruins, always in the playoffs under Clapper, missed the postseason scramble the following year.

In Fort George, British Columbia, a few years ago, I encountered Clapper's son Don managing a fast-food outlet. Was Don a player in his youth? "Yes, but not a star like my dad. The highlight of my junior career was being invited to the training camp of the Barrie Flyers. And guess who my roommate was — Don Cherry. Cherry made the club and I didn't."

Don Clapper talked about his father's strength and stamina. He mentioned the time his father was seriously injured one season.

"He severed a tendon in a game and it was a horrible injury. It required 100 stitches inside and another 100 stitches outside the wound. The doctors said he might never skate again, that he'd be lucky to be able to walk. Well, he was back on skates the following year. He was a tough and durable player. He had to be to survive twenty seasons in the NHL."

The young Clapper frowned when he recalled the time some-one suggested the Bruins bring his father's Number 5 out of retirement. "When the Bruins acquired Guy Lapointe from Montreal, Lapointe told them he wanted to wear his old number, Number 5. And the Bruins would have given it to him until my sister Marilyn, who lives back east, got involved. She made it very clear the family was not in favor of giving the number to Lapointe. Then Bobby Orr got involved. He supported my sister by saying, 'If they're going to unretire Number 5, which honors a Bruin who gave so much to the game, they might as well unretire Number 4.' I heard that Orr told Leo Monahan, the well-known Boston hockey writer, that Lapointe couldn't carry Clapper's jockstrap." The thought causes Clapper to chuckle, then add, "He's right, of course."

Clapper the Bruin was fast-tracked into the Hockey Hall of Fame in 1947 — two years before he retired as Boston coach. No one should be surprised when he's mentioned in the same breath as Orr and Bourque, Shore and Schmidt. He was that good.

Dit Clapper died in 1978.

Coutu Gets the Boot

BACK in 1927, a Boston player named Billy Coutu was handed hockey's stiffest penalty, a lifetime suspension.

On April 13, following a playoff game in Ottawa against the Senators — a game the Senators won to clinch the Stanley Cup — Coutu exploded in anger at referee Jerry Laflamme. He chased him down a corridor, pummeled him with punches, and knocked him to the floor. When Bill Bell, the linesman, hurried to the scene of the attack, he was thrown back, the victim of a flying tackle. NHL president Frank Calder, who was at the game, imme-diately handed Coutu a lifetime suspension plus a $100 fine.

The fine was deducted from Coutu's playoff share of $700. The lifetime ban was lifted five years later. By then Coutu, who'd been playing in the minors, and with fifteen years of pro hockey behind him, was too old to play in the NHL.

Hitchman an Unsung Hero

FROM 1923 to 1934 Lionel Hitchman was an elite defenseman in the NHL, a solid Bruin defender who never made an All-Star Team, never scored more than 11 points in a season, and, in retirement, never saw his name enshrined in the Hockey Hall of Fame.

Does he deserve to be there? Many oldtimers firmly believe he does. If he wasn't one of the best on ice, why would the Bruins retire his jersey?

Hitchman was never one to pull out his horn and begin tooting it. He was content to play in the shadow of colorful teammates like Eddie Shore, Dit Clapper, and Tiny Thompson — all Hall of Famers and worthy ones. Hitch was a classic stay-at-home defender who cleared the zone and protected his goalie. He made it hard on invaders. He made it easy for others to shine.

He came to the Bruins in a trade with Ottawa in January 1925 and if the Senators had known he would blossom overnight as a Bruin, they might never have let him go. He helped the Bruins to their first Cup final in 1927 (the B's fell in four games to the Senators) and led the Bruins to a first-place finish in the American Division the following year. That season he was named the club's first captain.

In 1928–29 Hitchman scored just one goal — his only point in 38 games. But he was so strong defensively, along with his fellow blueliners, that the B's gave up a mere 52 goals in 44 games. Goalie Thompson finished with a miniscule goals-against average of 1.18 and a dozen shutouts. "Without Hitch it would have been a different story," Tiny once said.

In ten years patrolling the Boston blueline, Hitchman led his mates to five first-place finishes in the American Division and three Cup finals.

The Hockey Hall of Fame often reaches back into the distant past to embrace an oldtime hero. Why not Lionel Hitchman, one of the best of the early Bruins?

Bruins Hockey Bewilders the Babe

SITTING in a box at the Boston Arena, next to the Chicago Blackhawks' bench, was the Sultan of Swat himself, Babe Ruth. The Babe had heard good things about a sport called hockey and he decided to see for himself what others were extolling. The game he chose to attend was one between the Boston Bruins and the Chicago Blackhawks on November 15, 1927. It turned out to be an ugly one.

The Babe, besieged by fans begging for autographs, could hardly stay focused on the game. But what did impress him was the hard body contact and, of course, the fighting.

At one point in the game, Eddie Shore was rubbed out along the boards. Shore got up, grabbed the puck, circled his own end, and took off like an enraged bull. He charged toward the Chicago end of the rink. He skated into two or three Hawks, sending them sprawling. He eventually lost the puck while going full speed and crashed into a sturdy Blackhawk defenseman, a collision which tossed both players violently to the ice.

After that incident, the Babe saw bodies flying all over the rink. He saw illegal high sticks and illegal elbows. He witnessed thundering checks and half a dozen fights. From his seat at rinkside he could hear the curses and the threats as tempers erupted and players charged into each other. He heard the howls and screams from 9,000 throats as the fans cried out for blood and vengeance.

The game ended in a 1–1 tie and the Babe made his way to the exits looking somewhat dazed and bewildered. He muttered to a companion, "Never saw anything like it. Those fellows wanted to kill one another. Thank God I'm in baseball. It's so peaceful and quiet."

2

Schmidt, Cowley, and Shore Become Stars

Football Farce at the Garden

ARDLY anybody remembers it — the day they played a football game at the Boston Garden. Maybe the slick promoter, Joe Alvarez, had the 1932 NFL championship in mind when he booked the arena for a game between Notre Dame Alumni and the "College All-Stars" on December 11, 1935. Three years earlier, on December 12, 1932, when a snowstorm blanketed Chicago on the day of the first NFL title game, the Chicago Bears met the Portsmouth Spartans indoors at the Chicago Stadium — on an 80-yard "field." With the hockey boards removed and six inches of dirt covering the floor of the arena, Chicago's Bronko Nagurski threw a pass to Red Grange for the only touchdown of the game.

For the 1935 game at the Boston Garden, Alvarez had trouble recruiting some of the best of the college boys — so he simply signed as many warm bodies as he could and gave some of them names of real players. Notre Dame star Frank Carideo, "One-Play" O'Brien and Temple's Al O'Neil — household names of the day — "played" in the game even though they never got within spitting distance of North Station.

The game was a farce from the outset.

Along with their paychecks, Alvarez promised the winning team a trip to Bermuda. But the players didn't believe him, nor did they have any faith in another Alvarez promise — that their paychecks would be waiting for them after the unique event.

The Notre Dame Alumni, trailing 6–0 at the half, refused to come out for the second half until Alvarez came up with their money. They knew a con man when they saw one.

"The man was used to dealing with professional wrestlers who weren't known for their brains," said Warren Casey, a Harvard grad who played in the game. "But he couldn't fool these college men."

Casey, who'd been a center at Harvard, volunteered to play for Alvarez. Despite receiving little acclaim during his college career, overnight Casey became a "Collegiate All-Star."

The fans who attended didn't like what they saw on the floor of the Garden. Throughout the game, they burst into mocking cheers. They chanted "We want Carideo" in reference to the Notre Dame star whose place in the lineup was filled by some anonymous imposter.

After Notre Dame registered a last-second 10–9 victory, Warren Casey called the novelty match a "once-in-a-lifetime experience. It was worth it," he said. "I never regretted playing in that farcical football game."

Hall of Fame
Inducts Conacher

SOME say the late Roy Conacher was a better hockey player than his famous brother — the Leaf's "Big Bomber," Charlie Conacher. But for half a century, the Hockey Hall of Fame's portals remained closed to Charlie's kid brother, despite his glowing credentials.

When the hall's selection committee finally took an in-depth look at Roy Conacher's NHL record, they agreed unanimously, "This guy was a star. Let's take him in." He was inducted in the Oldtimer's category on November 16, 1998.

Let's look at the newest Hall of Famer's career.

In 1935–36, a teenaged Roy Conacher starred for the West

Toronto Nationals in Junior hockey and led his team to a Memorial Cup championship.

The following season he played on a Senior championship club, the Dominion Breweries, and in 1937–38 he was a Northern Ontario Hockey Association All-Star, playing with a Kirkland Lake club.

In the fall of 1938, now 22, he attended the Boston Bruins training camp and easily won a spot on the team. As a rookie he led the NHL in goals with 26 and was a leading candidate for the Calder Trophy. But wouldn't you know, teammate Frank Brimsek, with 10 shutouts in 43 games, enjoyed a sensational rookie season and captured both the Calder and the Vezina. When the Bruins won the Stanley Cup over Toronto that season, Conacher scored the winning goal in the final game.

A broken wrist cost him 16 games the following season. He scored 18 goals in 31 games and helped the Bruins to another league championship.

In 1940–41, the Bruins topped the NHL standings again, losing only 8 games all season. Conacher led the club with 24 goals and helped linemate Bill Cowley win the Art Ross Trophy as scoring champion. During this season Boston set a league record with an undefeated streak of 23 games and went 15 straight games without losing on the road.

In 1941–42, Conacher scored another 24 goals but missed the next four seasons after signing up for military service in the Canadian Royal Air Force.

He returned with an honorable discharge and suited up for four regular season games and three games in the 1946 playoffs. In the off-season he was traded to Detroit because Boston manager Art Ross mistakenly believed he would never regain his pre-war form.

In 1945–46 with Boston, Conacher played on the same team as his nephew, Murray Henderson. With the Red Wings in 1946–47, playing on a line with Billy Taylor, Conacher led his team in goals with 30, a personal high. He was instrumental in helping Taylor set a league single-game assist record of seven. With Taylor assisting, Conacher scored four times in a 10–6 rout of Chicago on March 16, 1946. Incidentally, Taylor's record still stands.

Conacher was traded to Chicago prior to the following season. Despite missing several games because of injuries, he scored 22 goals. Midway through the season, he had the good fortune to be coached by his brother Charlie. In 1948–49, playing on a line with Doug Bentley and Bill Mosienko, Conacher won the NHL scoring title and the Art Ross Trophy with 26 goals and 68 points, two more than linemate Doug Bentley. Roy was named to the First All-Star Team.

During the 1949–50 season, Conacher scored his 200th career goal — the nineteenth player to reach that plateau. He played in the All-Star Game but his Blackhawks failed to make the playoffs.

Consistency was a Conacher trademark as he scored 26 goals the following season to lead his team. He was named to play in the 1951 All-Star Game but injuries kept him out of the lineup. He played 12 games at the start of the 1951–52 season and scored 3 goals. That gave him 226 career goals, one more than his illustrious brother. Perhaps his main objective that season was to finish ahead of Charlie. Once that was accomplished, he retired from the game.

Pusie Loved Penalty Shots

HE didn't have a long career in the NHL, and his stint with the Bruins amounted to a mere handful of games, but colorful Jean Pusie was a popular entertainer wherever he played. He was a character, a showman — a Stone Age Eddie Shack.

In Pusie's era, almost seventy years ago, the penalty shot was hockey's most dramatic play and Pusie, a husky French-Canadian, was convinced he excelled at the man-on-man challenge. It was an era when any player on a team could take the shot and Pusie was often selected not so much for his accurate shooting as for his flair for the dramatic.

He made each shot an event. First, he would stand at center ice and comb his thick hair. Then he would take a lengthy windup, skate slowly in on the waiting goaltender, stop in front of the nervous chap, take off a glove, and shake his hand. It was as if to say, "My poor fren'. I am ver' sorry I must now make you look embarras' in front of all these people."

Naturally, the crowd would be in an uproar. Hometown fans serenaded Pusie with a huge cheer, while in foreign rinks he'd hear deafening boos.

Another whirlwind windup would follow and this time Pusie would take his shot. If he missed and his detractors booed, he was known to circle the ice, find an opening, and leap in among the spectators, looking for those who dared to critique his penalty-shot performance.

Referee and Manager Battle

BOSTON fans had seen a lot of bizarre happenings in hockey but never anything like this. It was a ding-dong battle between a rival manager and a referee. There they were, slugging it out — two non-players tossing punches at each other in front of the visiting team's bench after the Bruins had scored a go-ahead goal.

It happened a long time ago, on the night of March 14, 1933, in a game between the Bruins and the Blackhawks at the Garden. The amazing rumpus began after Boston's Eddie Shore tied the score with two seconds on the clock. Then the Bruins' Marty Barry put the home team ahead 3–2 after three minutes of overtime, which in those days required ten minutes of extra play and was not sudden-death.

When Barry scored from a scramble, Chicago manager Tommy

Gorman exploded in anger. He accused the goal judge, Louis Reycroft, of flashing the red light before the puck had crossed the goal line. When referee Bill Stewart (the grandfather of current NHL referee Paul Stewart) passed the Chicago bench, Gorman reached out and grabbed him by the jersey.

Hot words were exchanged and Gorman began throwing lefts and rights at his smaller opponent. Stewart, who'd had many confrontations with baseball managers in his other vocation as a major-league umpire, hauled off and socked Gorman back. Gorman, dressed like a diplomat in his pearl-gray hat, gray coat, and pearl-gray gloves, began to haul Stewart's jersey over his head. But Stewart broke free and skated away from Gorman's flailing fists. He turned and shouted, "Yer outta here!" and ordered the Chicago manager to the dressing room. When Gorman refused to budge, police moved in and dragged him down the corridor.

The Blackhawks, loyal to their boss, left the ice with him. Some of them exchanged hot words with the gendarmes and were threatened with a stint in jail if they didn't back off. In the Chicago dressing room, Gorman told reporters, "Stewart hit me first. I was only retaliating."

Back on the ice, a fuming Stewart pulled out his watch and gave the Hawks one minute to get a lineup back on the ice. When they ignored his ultimatum, he forfeited the match to the Bruins. The two points picked up by the Bruins boosted them into a first-place tie with Detroit atop the NHL's American Division.

It was the first time in NHL history that a coach and his players had left the ice with the outcome of a game still in doubt. Referee Stewart refused to discuss the incident, except to say the penalty for such a breach of the rules meant forfeiture of two points and a $1,000 fine.

Ironically, four years later, Chicago owner Major Fred Mclaughlin hired Stewart to coach his hockey team. And guess what? The former referee guided them to the Stanley Cup in his first year behind the bench.

Roses for Ross

ART Ross and Leaf owner Conn Smythe were a couple of fierce competitors, always looking for the winning edge.

One night at the Boston Garden, Smythe received word that Ross was under the weather, suffering from one of those embarrassing anal irritations.

Smythe promptly ordered a dozen roses from a nearby florist and had them delivered to the Leaf dressing room. He then instructed King Clancy to skate across the ice to the Boston bench and deliver the bouquet to Ross. Along with the roses was an envelope.

"Be sure you read the card," Clancy said with a grin.

The Bruin manager ripped open the envelope, read the card, then tossed the roses into the nearest garbage can.

Smyth had written:

"Dear Art:

"Why Don't you take these roses and shove them up your sore ass."

Milt Schmidt Signs with Boston

MILT Schmidt first attracted interest from the Boston Bruins when he was a naive 17-year-old living in Kitchener, Ontario.

After being invited to the Bruins' training camp, the first

thing Milt did was write a letter to Bruins manager Art Ross saying that he would get a summer job to pay for the trip from Kitchener to the team's training base in Quebec. He didn't know the Bruins would provide all expenses. "Oh, I was green all right," Schmidt told me recently. "Especially when Ross called me in to sign my first contract with the Bruins. He offered me something like $3,000, and I told him I'd like $3,500. Well, he raised his eyebrows and said that was more than he'd been authorized to give me. He said he'd have to go down the hall and discuss my request with the team owner, Mr. Adams. So I waited patiently while he went to see Mr. Adams.

"In a few minutes he was back, and he had a grim look on his face. 'Sorry Milt,' he said, 'I fought for you, but Mr. Adams wouldn't budge on the $3,000 offer. He told me you could take it or leave it.'

"So I reached for a pen and signed the contract. On my way out of the building I passed Mr. Adams' office. I said to myself I think I'll go in there and ask Mr. Adams why he wouldn't give me the extra 500 bucks I requested. So I entered the office and encountered Mr. Adams' secretary.

"'Yes? Can I help you?' she asked.

"'Hi, I'm Milt Schmidt. I just signed with the Bruins and I'd like to see Mr. Adams, please.'

"She smiled and said, 'I'm sorry, but Mr. Adams isn't in today. He won't be in all week.'"

Milt turned to me. "Brian," he said, "they lied to me from day one and they have been lying to me ever since."

Top Defense Duo
Hated Each Other

EDDIE Shore and Babe Siebert made for an odd combination for the Bruins in the early 1930s. Siebert had been a big star for the Montreal Maroons for many years before joining Boston by way of New York. Perhaps Shore resented playing with a defenseman who was his equal — or almost so. It's more likely that they couldn't put past battles behind them.

Whenever the Maroons played the Bruins in that era, bloody donnybrooks invariably broke out — with Shore and Siebert always in the forefront. In a 1929 game at Montreal, Shore hit Seibert while the Maroons star was prone on the ice behind the Boston goal. Siebert, who suffered a broken toe, a number of bruised ribs, and a black eye, retaliated with fists and stick, sending Shore to the hospital with a broken nose, a concussion, and four missing teeth. Later in the season, Shore's fistic ability so impressed some boxing promoters that they offered him money to box Art Shires, an abrasive baseball player who fancied himself a pugilist. Shore was willing but Judge Landis, the commissioner of baseball, banned the proposed prizefight.

When Shore and Siebert teamed up in Boston in 1934, the animosity between them didn't cool. They never talked to each other. And yet, playing side by side on the Boston defense, they were as tough a combination as ever played the game. Herb Cain, who played with both the Maroons and the Bruins, once said, "It was like trying to fight your way through barbed wire to get to the Boston goal when those two were on the ice. Do you know Babe broke eleven thumbs in one year? He had a little chopping motion with his stick. As you were going by he'd give you a little chop on the hand with his stick. Not a full swing, just a six-inch swing. He broke so many thumbs the equipment manufacturers added a thumb guard to the gloves we wore. All because of Siebert.

"I cut around him one night and warded him off with my arm so he couldn't get at the puck. He hit me across the arm so hard the blow cut my elbow pad off. It paralyzed my arm. And it was just a six-inch chop. Man, he was strong! It was odd that he played so well with Shore when they despised each other."

Former Bruin Bill "Flash" Hollett once said, "Siebert wouldn't just cut you down. He'd send you straight to the hospital."

Siebert was a forward for most of his career, a key member of the famed "S" Line with the Maroons — Siebert, Hooley Smith, and Nels Stewart. After three years with Boston he wound up his career on defense for the Montreal Canadiens, where he was team captain for a further three seasons and a winner of the Hart Trophy in 1937. He was a moody, solemn figure, yet a loving husband to his wife, who became a helpless invalid after the birth of their second child. Medical expenses consumed most of his NHL salary. He retired from hockey in 1939 to take over as coach of the Canadiens. But on August 25, prior to training camp that year, he was cut down in the prime of his life, the victim of a drowning accident on Lake Huron. An All-Star Game in Montreal was played in Babe's memory and $10,000 from the proceeds went to his widow and his children.

Mel Hill Earns a Nickname

IN the mid-1930's, a 140-pound right winger from Glenboro, Manitoba, tried out unsuccessfully for the New York Rangers. The Ranger coaching staff said he was too light and he didn't have enough talent, but what Mel Hill lacked in size and talent he made up for in clutch ability.

Hill was not discouraged by the Ranger rejection. In fact, he expected it. He was, after all, a flyweight battling middleweights and heavyweights. He played amateur hockey for a year, added a few pounds, and by 1938 he caught on as a regular, not with the Rangers, but with the Boston Bruins. By the end of the season, it looked as if the rookie still was not ready for the fast pace of the National Hockey League. Hill managed only 10 goals for the entire season. With take-charge teammates like Eddie Shore, Dit Clapper, and Milt Schmidt, he appeared to be out of place on such a talented team. He considered himself fortunate indeed to hold down a spot on the Bruins' roster.

When the Bruins rolled into the playoffs that season, Hill was determined to make some kind of mark. He figured that a couple of solid playoff performances would go a long way toward ensuring future employment. Boston met New York in the semifinals. Hill thirsted for revenge on the club that had coldly turned him away only a few months earlier. In Game One, Hill scored a dramatic overtime goal to finish off a six-period marathon. In Game Two, Hill scored again in overtime to give the Bruins a 2–0 lead in the series. Boston took Game Three in regulation time and grabbed a commanding 3–0 lead in the series. But the Rangers, finally wide awake and furious, fought back with three straight victories to force a seventh and deciding game, to be played at the Boston Garden.

Game seven, a tight-checking, low-scoring affair, produced the most thrilling hockey of the series. The score was tied 1–1 going into overtime. That's when every Bruin fan in the building kept a close eye on Hill, hoping he could strike one more time with his overtime magic.

The first two overtime periods were scoreless. Late in the third extra frame, Hill took a Bill Cowley pass and slapped the puck past Rangers goalie Dave Kerr. Incredibly, he had done it again. His third overtime goal had captured the game and the series. By the following day, reporters and broadcasters across North America were referring to unheralded John Melvin Hill, the little winger from Glenboro, Manitoba, as Mel "Sudden Death" Hill, scoring hero of the Stanley Cup playoffs. The nickname would stick and become his sobriquet for the remainder of his life.

Hill's Bruins went on to win the Stanley Cup that year, defeating Toronto four games to one in the finals. When NHL president Frank Calder presented the Stanley Cup to Art Ross and the

Bruins on the ice at the Boston Garden, the fans roared for Eddie Shore, who had suffered a broken nose and a black eye in a play-off encounter with the Rangers' Muzz Patrick. The second loudest ovation went to Mel Hill, who was already anticipating bonus money amounting to $3,000. He pocketed $2,000 for the Stanley Cup win and a special bonus of $1,000 for his three over-time goals. The bonus money equaled his regular season earnings of $3,000. Not only did Hill gain his revenge on the Rangers, but he doubled his salary in the process.

Cowley's Record Snapped by Gretzky

BILL Cowley joined the Bruins in 1935–36 (after his rookie season with the St. Louis Eagles) and averaged over a point a game with them for the next dozen years. He was truly a remark-able player and a brilliant playmaker. In 549 regular-season games, he amassed 548 points, 353 of them assists. In the play-offs, 34 of his 46 points in 64 games were assists.

It was often said that Cowley made more wings than Boeing. Mel Hill, Eddie Wiseman, Roy Conacher, Charlie Sands, Ray Getliffe, Herb Cain, Art Jackson, Buzz Boll, Busher Jackson, Terry Reardon, and Kenny Smith were among the grateful wingers who benefited from Cowley's magic wand. He could feather passes to their waiting sticks much the same way that Gretzky has done for his many mates over the past two decades.

In the 1939 playoffs, Mel Hill, a mediocre winger, would not have received his famous nickname — "Sudden Death" Hill — if it hadn't been for Cowley. The Ottawa native set up all three of Hill's game-winning overtime goals in the semifinals against the New York Rangers. Cowley did most of the work while Hill earned all the glory — and a popular new monicker. Cowley led all play-off scorers that year with 3 goals and 11 assists in 12 games. During the regular season, he scored a mere 8 goals but his league-leading 34 helpers placed him third in the scoring race behind Toe Blake of Montreal and Sweeney Schriner of the New York Americans.

Teammate Flash Hollett once said of Cowley, "He would stick-handle down the ice and zero in on an opposing defenseman. He wasn't fast on his feet but that puck was glued to his stick. Somehow he seemed to freeze the defenseman in one spot while he cut across — into the center. His two wingers — often it was Hill on one side and Roy Conacher on the other — would dart in behind the defensemen, who were worried about Cowley. What was *he* going to do? Well, he knew what he was going to do. He'd feather a pass in between them, right onto the stick of one of his wingers. And they'd be home free. Nobody passed any better than Cowley. He was a pleasure to watch when he made those beautiful passes."

Cowley was proudest of a record he set during the 1943–44 season. He was having one of his most productive seasons and jumped ahead of everybody in the scoring race, collecting 53 points by January 7, 1944. Then it happened. During a game between Toronto and Boston, the Leafs' Jackie McLean sent Cowley crashing into the boards, separating his shoulder. The injury kept him out of the lineup for a month. He was back on the ice by mid-February, but was sidelined again with another injury, this time to his knee.

That season, he ended up with 71 points in just 36 games. This gave him an average of 1.97 points per game. The record stood for more than 38 years. It took Wayne Gretzky, the NHL's all-time points leader, to break the mark in 1981–82 when he scored an all-time high 212 points, averaging 2.65 points per game.

Only two players have consistently averaged more than two points per game in a season: Gretzky and Mario Lemieux. For Cowley to remain third on the list, after more than half a century — setting a mark that great sharpshooters like Phil Esposito, Bobby Hull, Gordie Howe, Steve Yzerman, and Bobby Orr have been unable to surpass — is truly remarkable.

I played against Cowley one night in Ottawa in the early 1950s. He was at least 40 by then. Our Junior A team was involved in an exhibition game with a team of NHL Oldtimers and Cowley was the best man on the ice. I recall how impressed we were when he slipped the puck through a tiny crack between our goaltender's pad and the goal post. It was the smallest opening imaginable but Cowley spotted it and slipped the puck through it. I remember he grinned at us as he turned away, as if to say, "That's how I used to do it with the Bruins."

Brimsek Makes a Sensational Debut

WHEN the Boston Bruins sold goalie Tiny Thompson to Detroit in 1938, some of the Bruins thought it was a shame, a bonehead mistake. Thompson, a 10-year veteran, had won four Vezina Trophies and was extremely popular with the fans and his teammates. Defenseman Dit Clapper, Thompson's roommate, was so incensed when he heard of his pal's departure that he threatened to quit the game on the spot.

"Art Ross will never be able to replace Tiny," the skeptics agreed. "The man must be losing his marbles."

But the replacement Ross had in mind, a kid from Minnesota named Frank Brimsek who'd been playing in Providence, made such a sensational debut in the Boston goal that fans and players alike, within days, grudgingly agreed that he performed even better than Thompson.

In his third game against Montreal, Brimsek was unflappable and made a dozen brilliant saves. Still, the Bruins lost 2–0.

In his next seven starts, Brimsek embarked on a streak that astonished the world of hockey. It began with a 5–0 shutout of the Blackhawks in Chicago. Two nights later, he blanked Chicago again by a 2–0 score. He followed up with a 3–0 shutout over the Rangers. In his seventh NHL game, he broke Thompson's record for shutout minutes when the Bruins edged Montreal 3–2. In his next three games, he was unbeatable. He blanked the Canadians 1–0, the Red Wings 2–0, and the Americans 3–0.

By then Boston fans were calling Ross a genius and they'd picked out a proper nickname for their new goalie — Mr. Zero. It would stick with him for the rest of his life.

After compiling 6 shutouts in seven games, Brimsek and the Bruins were shut down themselves. They lost 1–0 to the Rangers.

But Brimsek's amazing start was no fluke. He went on to win the Calder Trophy that season (with 10 shutouts and a 1.59 goals-against average). He also captured the Vezina Trophy, a berth on the First All-Star Team, and saw his name engraved on the Stanley Cup when the Bruins eliminated the Leafs four games to one in the finals.

Wartime hostilities robbed Brimsek of two NHL seasons, 1943–44 and 1944–45. He tended guns instead of goal nets on a patrol boat in the South Pacific. He was not as sharp when he returned because "walking those decks for two years was hard on my feet. My legs were never the same again after the war."

Harold Kaese, then a Boston columnist, would write glowingly of Brimsek: "If all the pucks stopped by Frigid Frankie were stuck together, they would form a solid rubber hose, three inches in diameter, one that would stretch from Boston to his home in Minnesota."

His home was in Virginia, Minnesota, five miles from the U.S. Hockey Hall of Fame in Eveleth, where a plaque honors his memory and his achievements. He was inducted into the Hockey Hall of Fame in Toronto in 1966.

Mr. Zero died of a heart attack while preparing to shovel snow on November 11, 1998.

Eddie Shore's Quirks

WHEN Bruin Hall of Famer Eddie Shore bought the Springfield hockey club many years ago, he became known for running the club in a unique fashion.

Don Cherry, who played under Shore, tells some fascinating stories about Shore's quirks and bizarre behavior. As the owner, player, and coach, just before game time, Shore could be seen parking cars outside the Springfield Arena. Then he'd dash inside, suit up, and play for his team.

There's a story, difficult to believe, that Shore instructed his players never to tip a cab driver more than fifteen cents. Soon, no cabbie would pick up a Springfield hockey player. If a player had a bonus clause for scoring 30 goals, Shore would bench him when he neared the mark.

Shore insisted that his players practice tap dancing in hotel lobbies and ballet moves on the ice. He assured one player that he would score more often if he combed his hair differently. He tied another player's legs together because he felt the player was skating with his legs too far apart. He tied his goalies to the crossbar to teach them to remain standing upright during game action. At least once he locked a referee in the officials' dressing room because he felt the man had done a poor job during the game.

He told his players that he had cured himself of cancer and that he had survived eight heart attacks in efforts to promote his special treatments and home remedies to sick or injured players. He enjoyed displaying his chiropractic skills. "You'd ache for a week after he finished working on you," says Cherry. "Some players were terrified to get on that medicine table."

Once, Shore invited all of the players' wives to the arena. They dressed for the occasion, thinking he had planned a surprise party for all of the players. When the women arrived, Shore sat them down and preached to them his views on sex. He instructed them to "be celibate until the playoffs are over," because "too much sex" was the reason for the Indians' poor play.

He destroyed the dreams of many players who quit the game rather than play for him. Players around the league referred to Springfield as the Siberia of hockey. When they signed their contracts with other clubs, they added a clause that prohibited a trade to Springfield.

Once, Shore desired a goalie by the name of Smith. He made the trade and awaited the arrival of the newest member of his team. When Smith entered the Springfield dressing room, Shore said, "Where are your goalie pads?" The puzzled Smith replied, "But I'm not a goalie, I'm a forward."

Leave it to Shore to trade for the wrong Smith.

There's a story of a famous playoff incident involving Shore that Leaf Hall of Famer King Clancy enjoyed telling:

"In March of 1936 we played the Bruins in the playoffs. In those days it was a two-game series, highest score to win. Well, the Bruins blanked us 3–0 in Boston, and in the second game back in Toronto they jumped to a 1–0 lead. It looked like curtains for the Leafs.

"Shore was the big cheese of the Bruins so I decided to try a little goading. I told my mates when we left the dressing room for the second period, 'Don't worry. I got Shore in my hip pocket.' After the period started, Shore was caught for some infraction and that made him mad. He was headed for the penalty box when I intercepted him and said, 'Geez, Eddie. That was a rotten call. Are you gonna let the referee get away with that?'

"My words must have influenced him because he wheeled around, laid his stick on the puck and fired it at the referee, Odie Cleghorn. Cleghorn wouldn't stand for that sort of nonsense and sent Shore off with an additional ten-minute misconduct penalty. Boston was a different team without him. By the time he got back, we'd tied the score overall and eventually went on to beat the Bruins 8–6 on total goals."

"Another time," added Clancy, "I nailed Shore into the boards and he didn't like it one bit. He turned in a flash and raised one big mitt, ready to let me have it. I grabbed his glove and pumped his arm up and down. I said, 'Hello, Eddie. How are you tonight?' And he mumbled, 'Pretty good, King. Pretty good.'"

Clancy continued, "Did you know Shore used to come out on the ice for the warmup in Boston wearing a long gold dressing gown over his uniform? And the music would blare out 'Hail to the Chief' while he skated around with those long strides of his. The Boston crowd loved it. One night I skated up next to him and said, 'I hope you're gonna wear that gown in the game tonight, Eddie. You look so lovely in it. Trouble is, you'll probably get all tangled up in it, fall into the boards and then start crying for a penalty.'"

"He just glared at me and said, 'I'll kill you tonight, Clancy.'"

"I laughed and said, 'You try it, Eddie, if you don't mind taking a good licking right in front of all of your fans.'"

"How I loved to needle Shore. He was a fabulous hockey player and later on he became a good friend of mine."

The Eddie Shore– Ace Bailey Incident

DECEMBER 12, 1933, was a black day in the history of Boston hockey. A check delivered in anger — and from behind — by Bruin tough guy Eddie Shore ended an opponent's career and left him near death with a fractured skull. It remains one of hockey's greatest tragedies.

There was little evidence of Christmas spirit in the stands or on the ice that night. The largest crowd of the season howled for blood as they watched the Bruins and the Leafs pound each other from the opening whistle. Before long there would be pools of blood on the ice and many would be forced to turn away, sickened at the sight.

In the second period, Eddie Shore made one of his patented rushes and was tripped up by King Clancy at the Toronto blue-line. Clancy grabbed the puck from Shore and made a dash of his own into the Boston zone. Meanwhile, Shore had jumped to his feet and targeted the nearest Leaf for a return check. The innocent opponent was Ace Bailey, who had his back to Shore.

Frank Selke, Toronto's assistant general manger, was sitting in the front row of the press box, in perfect position to see what happened next. He would write in his memoirs, "Shore arose and slowly started back for his end of the playing arena. He was behind [Red] Horner and Bailey. Whether he mistook Bailey for Clancy, or whether he was annoyed by his own futility and every-thing in general, nobody will ever know. But we all saw Shore put his head down and rush at top speed. He struck Bailey across the kidneys with his right shoulder and with such force that it upended Bailey in a backward somersault, while the powerful Shore kept right on going."

Bailey's head hit the ice with terrific force, fracturing his skull in two places. An awestruck hush fell over the arena. Everyone realized immediately that Bailey, his knees raised, his body quiv-ering, was very badly hurt. Clancy would say, "I had many battles with Shore but I never thought he was a vicious player. He wasn't out there to maim anybody. But that night he cer-tainly hit Bailey as hard as he could. It was a shocking thing to see."

Toronto's Horner, a muscular defenseman, skated past his unconscious teammate, then made a beeline for Shore, who stood as though stunned. He took Shore by the shoulders, then pole-axed him with a right to the jaw. Shore collapsed to the ice, out cold. Blood flowed freely from a deep cut to his head and spread across the ice.

Bailey and Shore were carried to their respective dressing rooms. In the visitors' room, Bailey began convulsing. His head was packed in ice and then, barely conscious, he was rushed to a Boston hospital. Two delicate brain operations in the next ten days were necessary to save his life. Even when the crisis passed, doctors were concerned about permanent damage to the brain that might result from such a severe concussion. The Leaf forward never played hockey again but he made a satisfactory recovery and lived to a ripe old age.

While the two injured players were being carried off that night, the Boston crowd, for no good reason, became ugly. Many left their seats and jammed the corridors. Toronto manager Conn Smythe, taunted by some as he fought his way to the dressing room, lashed out and punched a fan. Smythe was later hauled into court and charged with assault. But a sympathetic judge ruled that his actions were the result of great stress and all charges were dismissed.

Back in Toronto on the night of the incident, Bailey's father, having listened to Foster Hewitt's description of the incident on the radio, grabbed a revolver and hopped a train to Boston. He fully intended to shoot Eddie Shore — if he could find him. But Smythe and Frank Selke intercepted the elder Bailey and plied him with liquor until he was in no condition to shoot anybody. They relieved him of his gun, then slipped him aboard a train headed back to Canada.

Shore's head wound required several stitches. He left for Bermuda a few days later, after learning that he'd been suspended for 16 games.

Two benefit games were held for Bailey. The Bruins announced that all the profits from a Boston–Montreal Maroons game on December 19 would go into a fund for Bailey. But a modest turnout at the gate produced little more than $6,000. Two months later in Toronto, a game between the Bruins and the Leafs brought the stricken star another $25,000.

"I bought a house with that money," Bailey once told me, "and had plenty left over."

It was during the pre-game ceremonies at the benefit game in Toronto that Eddie Shore approached Bailey for the first time since the incident at the Boston Garden. Tentatively, he skated up to Bailey and offered his hand. Bailey smiled. His firm handshake convinced the crowd he held no grudge against his adversary. Shore was forgiven. The Toronto fans roared at this display of sportsmanship. At rinkside, a number of Toronto's finest sighed in relief; they had anticipated an ugly demonstration, perhaps even a riot.

Shore wasn't much use to himself or his teammates for the rest of that season. In fact, almost a year passed before he displayed his old dynamic fury.

James Hendy, a writer of that era, once said of Shore, "It is doubtful that any player will ever equal Shore's efficiency in capitalizing on his bad man reputation. The NHL fixed an annual salary maximum which many players have exceeded, but Shore is the only one who forced the league to wink at more than double the figure."

War-Time Hockey and
Another Stanley Cup

Bitter Memories of Boston

HERB Cain enjoyed thirteen seasons in the NHL as a left winger with the Montreal Maroons and the Boston Bruins. In 1945–46, playing for the Bruins, he scored his 200th career goal, an impressive total in that era. At 33, he felt he could play for two or three more years. But his boss, Art Ross, felt otherwise. He decided Cain was too old for the NHL, even though two other NHL clubs coveted his services. Both the New York Rangers and the Chicago Blackhawks tried to buy him from the dictatorial Ross.

"I know you can make the Bruins again," Ross told Cain. "But you're not going to. I'm sending you to Hershey in the American league. You're finished in the NHL."

"If Boston doesn't want me, there are four other clubs in the NHL that'll take me in a minute," Cain replied. "Two of them just tried to buy me from you."

"Doesn't matter," Ross said. "You're going to Hershey and that's it."

"I was bitter because that was the year they brought in the pension," Cain recalled. "I would have been eligible if I'd played with Boston another season. And I was bitter because Ross sent me to Hershey on condition Hershey would not sell me to another NHL club. The NHL was like a little house league then. The six owners simply made up their own rules, called each other up and made deals, and settled things among themselves. The players had no clout, no say in anything.

"One year in Boston I held out for more money. The word soon got out that Cain was holding out. Nobody was to speak to him. I met Hap Day on the street and he walked right by. Didn't even say hello. If a player holds out today the other teams jump in and try to make a deal for him. In my day the holdout was a leper. Those six owners really stuck together. Players in my day had to toe the line or else. Today's players have too much say. It's gone from the ridiculous to the sublime.

"They could do that then. They had all the power and control. That's the reason I never played in the NHL again. A few years ago, some of my friends, fellows I'd played with in the NHL, tried to get me into the Hockey Hall of Fame. Maybe if I'd played a couple of years more with Boston, or any club, I would have made it.

"Art Ross was a funny guy. He lived in a little world all his own. One time Woody Dumart got hurt and the Boston paper said that Cain would replace him on the Kraut Line. It went on to say that Ross would bring up Hamill to take Cain's place. I laughed when I read it and told my wife, 'There's no way the paper is going to tell Ross what to do. I'll wager he plays Hamill on the Kraut Line and I'll be playing where I always play.' And of course that's exactly what happened."

A Goalie from Heaven

T HE Bruins arrived in Toronto on a November day in 1943 without a goaltender. Bert Gardiner, a replacement for Frank Brimsek who had gone to war, was ill with influenza. Manager Art Ross, scrambling for a replacement for Gardiner, was told that George Abbott, the Leafs' practice goalie and an ordained minister, would be worth looking at. "I'll give him a try," he said. "Maybe Heaven will be on his side."

Abbott, a Hamilton native, had nearly lost his eye to a puck three years earlier and had not played competitively since the injury. Still, he jumped at the chance to play in the NHL. But after he gave up a raft of goals in a 7–4 loss to the Leafs, Abbott's big-league career was over.

"I don't think I ever tried so hard in my life to play well in goal," he said after the match. "And the Leafs never played better than they did tonight. Too bad it had to be against me.

"You know, three of the goals were actually scored by Bruins. Flash Hollett deflected one off his glove into my net. Then, when he tried to clear a puck he missed it and a Leaf player scored. Then Dit Clapper had a puck deflect off his stick and it fell into my net. And all the time I was trying my best to give Boston the best goaltending I could.

"Oh, well, it was a lot of fun. I just hope folks don't think I wasn't trying. I must have been for they tell me I stopped 46 shots."

When the Bruins were asked about the performance of Reverend Abbott, Dit Clapper said, "He did all right. Sure, he was a bit nervous, but who wouldn't be? When he was getting dressed for the game, I had to tell him he was putting his skates on the wrong feet. And I warned the guys not to curse and swear around him. But just as we were going out for the warmup, one of the Bruins forgot. He banged him on the shoulder and said, 'Don't worry, George. We'll whip those bastards for you.'

"I guess the funniest thing he did was turn to look into the net for a puck. But it wasn't there. Before he could turn back around, someone hit him right in the ass with a shot. It may have been his best save of the game."

Cowley's Sporting Gesture

WILLIAM Miles Cowley was one of the NHL's all-time great playmakers. He played on two Stanley Cup championship teams, was voted to the First All-Star Team four times — and once to the Second All-Star Team — and he received several individual awards, including the Art Ross Trophy in 1941 and the Hart Trophy twice, in 1941 and 1943. He was inducted into the Hockey Hall of Fame in 1968.

During the 1943 NHL season, Bill Cowley displayed a remarkable bit of sportsmanship. He was on track to break his own record of most assists in a season (45), set in 1941. After a game between Boston and the Rangers one night, Cowley sent a letter to NHL president Red Dutton.

He wrote:

On January 16, during a game played here [at Boston] against the Rangers, Art Jackson was awarded a goal when Warwick threw his stick to prevent a goal. The official scorer has credited me with an assist, for having made the play which put Jackson in a scoring position. I feel that this assist was not justified, owing to the fact that Jackson did not actually score the goal, it was awarded as a result of the foul called on the Ranger player. Therefore, may I ask that you eliminate the assist credited to me from your next official scoring summary.

Yours truly,
Bill Cowley

Dutton, a former player himself, had never heard of a player asking to have a point deducted from his scoring record. But he granted Cowley's request. A perfect ending to the story would have seen Cowley win the Art Ross Trophy as scoring champion. And a bonus was waiting for him if he established a record for most assists in a season. Unfortunately, neither happened. Cowley finished second in the individual scoring race with 72 points, one behind Chicago's Doug Bentley. And the point he refused to accept on the Jackson goal cost him a new record for assists. He lost his bonus when he merely tied his previous league mark of 45. The extra point was notable when he retired in 1947, because his career total of 548 points was just one point less than the number of games he'd played — 549.

Flaman Had a
Sense of Humor

FERDINAND "Fern" Flaman enjoyed every minute of his 15-year career in the NHL. A defenseman from Dysart, Saskatchewan, Flaman joined the Bruins for a game in 1944–45, played in another game the following season, and became a Bruin regular in 1946–47. He was traded to Toronto in 1950, was dealt back to the Bruins in 1954, and retired from NHL play after the 1960–61 season.

While most Bruin fans remember Flaman for the way he punished opposing forwards, game officials remember him for his practical jokes and his sense of humor.

Referee Red Storey was officiating in Boston one night and handed out a penalty to one of the Bruins. Flaman skated over and went nose-to-nose with Storey, staring him straight in the eye and breathing foul air in the redhead's face. Finally Storey said, "What's the matter, Flaman, can't you talk? And why are you breathing all over me?" Flaman's answer was priceless: "Red," he growled. "I've got the lousiest cold in Boston and I'm standing here until you catch it."

On another night, Neil Armstrong, a rookie linesman, was trying to break up a fight at the Garden. The stringbean official grabbed Flaman by the arm and pulled him away from the melee. Flaman cried out, grabbed his arm, and, while it flopped at his side, he turned on Armstrong. "Look what you've done! You've broken my arm. Who let you into the league, kid?" He howled in mock pain while his arm did a dance of its own.

Armstrong was aghast. In his very first game, he'd seriously injured one of the game's best players. He was so upset he couldn't speak. Seconds later, when the grimace on Flaman's face changed into a big grin, the linesman knew he'd been the victim of a practical joke. Neil Armstrong remembers little else about his first game in the NHL. But he'll never forget Flaman's little caper.

Bruins Capture '41 Cup in Record Time

ON April 12, 1941, the Boston Bruins established a new Stanley Cup record with an easy victory over Detroit in the Cup finals. The Bruins won in four straight games, an unprecedented accomplishment.

The Bruins prepped for the playoffs by running up a 23-game undefeated streak during the regular season. After dropping a 2–0 decision to the Rangers on February 25, which ended the streak, the Bruins went undefeated in their remaining seven games.

The Bruins met Toronto in a semi-final playoff round and ousted the Leafs in seven games. Herb Cain had two game-winning goals and Mel Hill scored the winner in Game Seven, a 2–1 victory at the Boston Garden.

In the finals against Detroit, after the Red Wings suffered through three consecutive losses by scores of 3–2, 2–1 and 4–2, Red Wing fans showed little support for their team for Game Four at the Olympia. Only 8,125 showed up — half as many as witnessed the first two games at the Boston Garden. They were distressed when Red Wing enforcer Jimmy Orlando took a second period penalty. The Bruins promptly pumped in two goals while he rested in the box. The final score was 3–1 for the Bruins. It was the second time in three years that Boston had captured the Cup and the first time a four-of-seven series had been completed in the minimum number of games.

There was a brief presentation at center ice following the game. Handshakes were exchanged and then the champions headed for the railroad station where they caught the train back to Boston.

Krauts Go to War

ON February 11, 1942, the Bruins' famous Kraut Line of Milt Schmidt, Woody Dumart, and Bobby Bauer received an emotional send-off at the Boston Garden following a pasting of the Montreal Canadiens.

After the Bruins racked up 22 points in goals and assists (the Kraut Line accounted for half of them) in an 8–1 thrashing of the Habs, it was time to say goodbye to the boys — they had signed up for active service with the Royal Canadian Air Force. Applause filled the building as the three linemates were presented with paychecks for the remainder of the season — plus a handsome bonus.

There were words of praise from team manager Art Ross who thanked the remarkable trio for their outstanding play over the years. Ross wished them godspeed in the much bigger battles that lay ahead.

Then, putting bitter rivalries aside, the Montreal players joined the Bruins in hoisting the three air force recruits onto their shoulders and carrying them to the exit. It was a rare and dramatic moment in Bruin history. Tears spilled down several thousands of cheeks as the boys, three of the most popular players ever, waved farewell to their fans.

Don Gallinger's Suspension

"**W**E were in Toronto for a game when it happened. We were called into a hotel suite and told that Gally had been suspended and that he might never play hockey again. The players were absolutely shocked."
— *Murray Henderson, Boston defenseman*

In late February 1948, NHL President Clarence Campbell suspended Bruins' center Don Gallinger from hockey for the rest of his life.

At the age of 22, Don Gallinger made a huge mistake. A gambler, and not a very good one according to Murray Henderson, he became involved in wagering on the outcome of hockey games. It began innocently enough. A few meetings, a couple of handshakes, and the exchange of telephone numbers. First the bets were small. But as they grew in size, they grew in frequency and soon the debts began to pile up. The final bet he made was a $1,000 wager on a game between the Chicago Blackhawks and the Boston Bruins. Ironically, Gallinger's line scored the tying goal and his Bruins won the game. Gallinger lost the bet.

"No one knew what I was doing," said Gallinger. "Sure I bet, I admit that, but I never fixed a game, never tried to. It was so strange sitting on the bench in those games. You tried not to let it affect you, but of course it does."

Gallinger, a five-year Bruin veteran, was caught after police in Michigan became involved in an unrelated case. During an investigation, Gallinger and ex-teammate Billy Taylor of the Rangers were identified as clients of bookmaker and racketeer James Tamer.

On February 24, 1948, NHL President Clarence Campbell began an intensive investigation on behalf of the league and two weeks later announced that Gallinger and Taylor would be dealt lifetime suspensions from hockey because of their association with known gamblers. Campbell emphasized that no other players were involved and that no fix of a game had been attempted.

Taylor confessed to the charges while Gallinger chose to deny everything. Neither player had a legal representative at the hearing in front of Campbell. The sentence appeared to be unusually harsh in light of similar evidence in a case two years earlier involving Toronto's star defenseman Babe Pratt.

Pratt admitted to wagering on NHL games when questioned by Red Dutton, Campbell's predecessor as league president. Pratt also confessed that he'd been offered money to throw a game. Pratt's expulsion came on February 29, 1946. He was reinstated on March 14, thanks largely to Dutton's appeal to the NHL governors for leniency. Pratt went on to enjoy a Hall of Fame career.

Gallinger and Taylor were less fortunate. They were banished from the game in disgrace, their livelihood gone, their reputations shattered. Finally, in 1971, the NHL forgave them their trespasses and lifted the most severe penalties in NHL history. Taylor returned to the NHL as a scout. Gallinger claims nobody would hire him, not even his old teammate Milt Schmidt, who was then running the Washington Capitals.

Equipment Woes in the Forties

DEFENSEMAN Murray Henderson joined the Bruins as a regular in 1945 and played with them for eight seasons. He chuckles when he thinks of what Boston hockey was like in those days.

"First, if you were a rookie on the team, you expected to get some pretty fancy equipment, right? Everybody was thrilled to get a pair of new skates. After that it was a scramble. Win Green, the trainer, had a kind of loft over the dressing room and he'd climb up there and grab equipment that must have dated back to the turn of the century. And he'd start tossing it down. A new kid might get a pair of Lionel Hitchman's old shin pads or a pair of Eddie Shore's old shoulder pads smelling of mildew. You could see the rookies thinking, I wore better than this in junior hockey. One of our stars, Bill Cowley, was always nursing hand or wrist injuries and I think it was because the gloves he'd been given didn't offer much protection from all the slashes he took.

"Sweaters, or jerseys as they call them today. We got one and it was often well-worn and patched and stitched together where the holes appeared. Home and away sweaters were still a long way off when I joined the team. The stockings also had lots of holes in them and they'd been patched up. Still, it was a major league uniform and nobody complained, at least not out loud. We were in the NHL and we were all proud to wear it.

"And you wouldn't dare give a stick or even a puck away. Win Green kept track of all this stuff and he had orders to keep expenses to a minimum. Word spread around the league that Boston and Montreal spent less on equipment, and got more mileage out of it, than any other club.

"If our skates needed sharpening a man came around with a big bag and collected them. He took them to the Boston Arena where they had a skate sharpener. It's hard to believe we didn't have one in the Garden. If you nicked your skate blade in a game, you relied on a stone to smooth it out.

"I enjoyed the bridge games on the road trips. I remember once Johnny Peirson and I were ordered to report to Mr. Ross's compartment. That was never a good sign. We thought we'd been traded. When we got in there, it turned out he and Lynn Patrick, the coach, wanted us to play bridge with them.

"And years later, when Mr. Ross offered me a coaching position in Hershey I hesitated to accept. I told him I'd never been a coach before.

"He laughed and said, 'Anybody who can play bridge like you can won't have any trouble coaching hockey.' So I accepted his offer."

Milt Was a Superstar

HERB Cain, who played for the Boston Bruins from 1939–40 through 1945–46, says that many players of his era would have selected Milt Schmidt as the best all-round player in the NHL.

"Schmidt was a terrific player," Cain said. "In fact, he was the best player I ever played with or against. He could slow a whole team down all by himself. I never saw a forward who could bodycheck the way he could. I remember one night we were playing the New York Americans and by the end of the second period Schmidt had put three guys out of the game with his crushing checks. Finally, Flash Hollett came over and asked him to 'stop bodychecking, for Pete's sake,' so we can 'get the damn game over with.'

"Schmidt often skated with his head down so you'd think he was going to get clobbered. I mean, hockey's supposed to be a heads-up game, right? Then, all at once, he'd leave his feet and spring at the guy who was going to lay a big hit on him. Schmidt would nail the fellow before he was ready and the guy's stick would go one way and his body the other. I never saw anyone like him. I've seen many a fellow he hit stagger back to the bench like a guy coming home from an Irish wedding. The thing is, Milt wasn't that big — maybe 175 pounds. It's funny — you'd go for a walk with the guy and he'd wear glasses and move so slowly you'd think he was a preacher. But as soon as the puck was dropped, he was a regular tornado. When they name the all-time best of the Bruins, old Milt has to be right at the top of the list."

Fiery Ted Lindsay agrees. The Hall of Fame left winger says, "Milt Schmidt was the greatest competitor I ever played against. He was a tremendous team player and a great skater. They can talk about the wonderful skaters in the game today all they want but those people never saw Milt in his prime. And tough! Why, he would come down on the right side and if he didn't make it through he would turn and come down on the left side. And if you stopped him there, he'd grab the puck again and this time he'd come down the middle and skate right on top of you. And he would hurt you. There were some jarring collisions when he did that. It took a brave person to stand in his way."

Schmidt played sixteen years with the Bruins, beginning in 1936–37 and retiring on Christmas day during the 1954–55 season. He quit to become coach of the Bruins, a position he held until 1960–61. He scored 229 goals and 575 points in 776 games. He was elected to the Hockey Hall of Fame in 1961.

Fireworks in the Fifties

The First Black Player

THEY called him the Jackie Robinson of hockey when the Boston Bruins called him up on January 18, 1958. He was Willie O'Ree, the first black player in the NHL, a fleet left winger from Fredericton, New Brunswick.

O'Ree was given a chance that was denied another black player a few years earlier. A Toronto youth, Herb Carnegie, should have been an NHLer. Everybody said so. But the Rangers refused to bring Carnegie to New York. And Toronto owner Conn Smythe once told him, "Herb, I'd sign you in a minute if I could turn you white."

So Willie O'Ree, not Carnegie, is remembered as the first black player to crack an NHL lineup.

O'Ree was born in Fredericton in 1935. He began skating at the age of three. In Junior hockey, playing for the Kitchener-Waterloo Canucks, he was struck in the face by a puck and lost 95 percent of his vision in one eye. He turned pro in 1956–57 with the minor-league Quebec Aces, signing for $3,500. He neglected to tell his employers he was legally blind.

O'Ree's first stint with the Bruins amounted to a mere two games — a home-and-home series with Montreal in January 1958. He recalls, "We beat the Habs at the Forum, 3–0, and back in Boston the following night they beat us 6–2. That was it. My two-game trial. By Monday I was back in Quebec City playing for the Aces, coached by Punch Imlach. I waited three and a half years before Boston called again."

During the 1960–61 season O'Ree was back with the Bruins, this time for 43 games. He scored 4 goals and added 10 assists.

The major difference between the NHL and the Quebec league was the number of racial slurs hurled at him by fans and other players. One night in Chicago he struck a Blackhawk over the head with his stick and a dozen fans sitting nearby threatened to lynch him.

"It started when Eric Nesterenko gave me a butt-end — right in the face. I spit out a couple of teeth and then nailed him over the head with my stick. The referee threw both of us out of the game but I needed police protection to get to the Boston dressing room. Those Chicago fans were livid. They were ready to murder me.

"They were mean to me in places like Detroit and New York, too. But never in Boston. I'll never forget how my teammates there — men like Johnny Bucyk, Doug Mohns, Charlie Burns, and Don McKenney — took care of me. They accepted me totally. All of them had class."

What did the first black player in the NHL earn? Not much. O'Ree recalls signing with the Bruins for an annual salary of $3,500 — precisely his salary in Quebec — plus a promise of a $200 bonus if he scored 20 goals.

And his best memory of the big league? "That's easy," he said. "I scored the winning goal against the Canadiens on January 1, 1961 — New Year's Day. I'll never forget the reception I got from the Boston fans when that puck went in."

The ovation lasted for more than two minutes, a well-earned salute to the first black player to score a goal in the NHL.

At the time it appeared that Willie was on his way. Milt Schmidt called him "one of the fastest skaters in the league." Lynn Patrick took him aside after the season: "Go home and have a good summer, Kid. We'll see you in training camp."

A few weeks later a reporter called. "Willie, what do you think about the deal?"

"Deal? What deal?"

"You've been sold to Montreal."

Oh, no, thought Willie. *Montreal is loaded with wingers. I'll never make that team.*

And he never did. But he was a minor-league star for years and won the Western Hockey League scoring crown twice.

"To this day a lot of people don't realize I played for twenty seasons while blind in one eye," he says.

On January 17, 1998, during ceremonies at the NHL All-Star Game, the NHL honored Willie O'Ree for his pioneering efforts and named him director of youth hockey development for the NHL/USA Hockey Diversity Task Force. He now travels all over North America helping kids from various backgrounds with their hockey skills and other life skills.

When Laycoe and the Rocket Collided

HAL Laycoe had always liked Rocket Richard. Before joining the Boston Bruins during the 1950–51 season, Laycoe had played for the Montreal Canadiens. He and Richard often played tennis together in the off season. They got along splendidly.

But during a game between the Habs and the Bruins at the Boston Garden on March 13, 1955, any goodwill between them was lost forever in a few violent seconds. "I hate to rehash the incident," Laycoe would say many times in retirement. "There was never anything like it. Ever."

Before his death at age 75 on April 28, 1998, Laycoe told Tom Hawthorn of the *Victoria Times-Colonist*, "The Rocket started the melee by pitchforking me in the face with his stick. I wore glasses and that's what saved me from a bad cut. I reached up and ding! I got him right in the back of the head. I remember Rocket touched his head. He saw blood and boy, did he come at me."

At that point Laycoe dropped his gloves and prepared to duke it out with the fiery Richard. But Richard had something else in mind. He swung his stick, nicked Laycoe's ear with it and crashed it down on the Boston player's shoulder. The stick splintered. Richard grabbed another stick and broke it over Laycoe's back. He picked up a third stick and attacked Laycoe, who said, "I was standing there like John L. Sullivan, fending off sticks with my hands and arms. The Rocket was relentless."

When linesman Cliff Thompson intervened, Richard punched the official twice.

The latter attack prompted NHL president Clarence Campbell to suspend the Montreal superstar for the rest of the season (three games) and the playoffs, a penalty that infuriated Richard's countless fans. When Campbell attended the Canadiens' next home game against Detroit, he was attacked by fans and pelted with debris. A tear gas container was thrown and exploded inside the Forum, the building was evacuated, and Detroit, leading 4–1, was awarded the victory. As the fans streamed out of the Forum, an angry mob indulged in a frenzy of looting and vandalism along St. Catherine Street. It was the blackest hour in Montreal hockey history.

Richard's suspension cost him his only chance to win the NHL scoring crown when teammate Boom Boom Geoffrion passed him in the final week of the season, edging ahead in points, 75–74.

Even without the Rocket, the demoralized Canadiens were able to oust the Bruins in five games in the semifinal round. Laycoe was vilified by Habs fans in the games played at the Forum and was told that the Montreal police were concerned about death threats against the Bruin defenseman. "I sat on the bench with a big Number 10 on my back," Laycoe told Tim Hawthorn. "If there was a nut with a gun in the stands, he'd have had a pretty good target." In the finals, the Habs lost to Detroit, four games to three. With the Rocket, they might have won the final series. If so, they would have embarked on a string of six consecutive Stanley Cup triumphs. They went on to rule as hockey's greatest team from 1956 through 1960.

Undoubtedly, Montrealers with long memories still swear the loss in '55 was all Hal Laycoe's fault.

Bruins Can't Stop
the Rocket

IN 1961, at the B'nai Brith Awards Dinner in Boston, three great athletes were honored as "history makers and competitors of high principle and achievement in sports." One was Dr. Roger Bannister, for beating the four minute mile; another was Rocky Marciano, the former world heavyweight champion, and the third was Maurice "Rocket" Richard, the recently retired NHL superstar.

Attendees at the dinner saluted the Rocket with a standing ovation. It was a departure from the boos and catcalls he'd heard so often from many of these same people whenever he'd played at the Boston Garden.

It was a night for reminiscing and the Rocket was asked to describe how he scored one of the greatest goals in Stanley Cup history. "I can't describe it," he laughed. "I was only half conscious when I scored that goal."

Longtime Bruin fans recalled the Rocket's brilliant goal, which killed Boston's Stanley Cup hopes in the spring of 1952. On the night of April 8, Boston and Montreal clashed at the Montreal Forum in the seventh game of a bruising semifinal series.

Richard, fresh from a team-sponsored trip to Florida, was a target for every Bruin throughout the series. And in Game Seven, they caught up with him. First he collided heavily with Bruins' winger Leo Labine. Then he crashed heavily into the knee of defenseman Bill Quackenbush, badly twisting his neck. The idol of French Canada lay prone on the ice for several minutes, blood flowing freely from a deep cut on his forehead. Someone called for a stretcher and he was carried off while the Forum crowd booed Quackenbush.

Boston fans were elated to have the Rocket *hors de combat*. They figured he was gone for the rest of the game, greatly enhancing their chances of winning the Stanley Cup. But they were wrong. In the Montreal dressing room, the Rocket began to regain his senses. He had six stitches in his head, he was groggy, and the team doctor advised him to take off his equipment, shower, and go home.

The Rocket simply stared down at the floor. "Give me a few minutes. I'll be all right," he muttered.

The third period was under way when he got up, shook off some of the cobwebs, and staggered back to the Montreal bench.

"How much time to go?" he asked Elmer Lach, his linemate.

"About four minutes, Rocket. And the score is tied 1–1."

Coach Dick Irvin hesitated. Should he let the Rocket back on the ice?

Richard glared at Irvin. "I'm all right. I can play," he said.

Irvin changed lines and the Rocket skated out. Seconds later, he took the puck behind his own net and embarked on a rush — one that would end in the greatest goal of his career. It was an electrifying dash that saw him stickhandle around or through the entire Boston team. After eluding all three forwards who tried to stop him, he swept around Bill Quackenbush at the Bruin blueline, warding him off with one hand. When Bob Armstrong raced over to cut him off, he button-hooked around the balding defenseman and came eye-to-eye with goalie Sugar Jim Henry.

Henry's face was marred by two black eyes and a broken nose, suffered earlier in the series. Prior to the game he could barely see. The team trainer had alternated placing hot and cold towels over his face to decrease the swelling and by game time he could see well enough to play. The Rocket's sight wasn't perfect, either. He had a blood-soaked patch over his left eye and a stream of blood slid down his cheek as he raced in on Henry. When Henry dove for the puck, the Rocket had just enough strength left to pull it back and snap it into the net.

The Habs won the contest 2–1, eliminating the despondent Bruins. But Henry showed lots of class. He skated up to the Rocket and shook his hand. A wonderful photo of that moment of sportsmanship has been printed a thousand times. Henry said, "I felt badly because we'd just been knocked out of the playoffs. But I felt compelled to congratulate the Rocket because it was such a beautiful goal — one of the best I've ever seen. There is no shame in losing to such a player. The Rocket filled areanas wherever he played in those days with the fans coming out to boo him or cheer him."

In the Montreal dressing room after the final whistle, the Rocket sat as if stunned. Then his body heaved in a violent convulsion. He trembled and sobbed and was placed on a table. A doctor rushed in and inserted a needle. Two hours later he was back to normal and was able to go home.

The following morning, the sports editor of the *Montreal Herald* wrote: "That beautiful bastard scored while semi-conscious."

Sugar Jim a Survivor

"HOW'D you get that name, Jim?" a reporter asked the goalie.

The Winnipeg native laughed and said, "I was always into our neighbor's sugar bowl when I was a kid. I've been Sugar Jim Henry ever since."

After playing junior hockey in Brandon and senior hockey in Regina, Henry guided the New York Rangers to a first place finish in the NHL in 1941–42.

Before the following season rolled around, he enlisted in the Canadian Army and 19 months later transferred to the Navy. He played on an Allan Cup–winning service team during the war — the Ottawa Commandos.

When he returned to the NHL three years later, the Rangers had no room for him. His old friend Charlie Rayner was New York's regular netminder. After playing in a handful of games over two seasons, Henry was traded to Chicago for 60 games and then moved to Detroit as part of a ten player deal. Former Red Wing goalie Harry Lumley, coming the other way in the trade, took his place in Chicago and rookie Terry Sawchuk barred his way from becoming a Detroit regular. After a stint in the minors, he was sold to the Bruins where he played for four seasons and didn't miss a game. The Bruins finished the 1952–53 season with a losing record and a mere 66 points but upset first place Detroit in the semi-finals. Henry was given most of the credit for the upset.

In the finals against Montreal, Henry twisted his ankle in the second game and was replaced by Gordon (Red) Henry (no relation), called up from Hershey. "I was getting treatment on the dressing room table when Red came rushing in. He'd cut his arm quite badly. The trainers threw me off the table and began working on him," Henry recalls.

After Red Henry allowed ten goals in games three and four (3–0 and 7–3) Sugar Jim was ready to play again. In Game Six he didn't allow a goal through three periods of play. But neither did Gerry McNeil at the other end of the rink. The teams played just over a minute of overtime when Elmer Lach intercepted a Milt Schmidt pass. Lach's quick shot glanced in off the right goal post and fell in behind Henry. The game and the series were over.

Henry's NHL career ended following a playoff game on March 31, 1955. He suffered a broken upper jaw when a puck off the stick of Montreal's Baldy Mackay hit him under the eye. He managed to finish the game (it went to two overtime periods) despite excruciating pain, then went straight to the hospital and three hours of surgery. His eyesight was never as sharp after the injury.

But his scariest moment came early in his career and a long way from a hockey rink. Henry, in partnership with Charlie Rayner, opened a fishing and hunting camp in Northern Ontario called Hockey Haven. One summer day in 1951 he was pouring gasoline to refuel a motorboat when an explosion lit up the shed in which he was standing. On fire from head to foot, Henry dashed out of the shed and rolled around on the grass to smother the flames.

When he saw the entire shed was afire, he dashed back into the building and tried to extinguish the blaze. For the second time, his clothes caught on fire. By then Rayner and others had arrived. They saved Henry and the building and then rushed Henry to hospital.

His body was so badly burned people said he'd never play

hockey again. But that fall, Art Ross failed to come to terms with goaltender Jack Gelineau (a Calder Trophy winner in 1950), and was in the market for an experienced goalie. He grabbed Henry despite the fact the netminder had been swathed in bandages for most of the summer. Ross never regretted it. The three seasons that followed were the best of Henry's career.

Talking with Topper

O N the golf course, Jerry Toppazzini is a delightful companion. Over eighteen holes in a charity tournament in Toronto he has lots of time to talk hockey — and his career with the Bruins (from 1952–53 through 1963–64 with brief stops in Detroit and Chicago).

"Did you know the Bruins alumni honored me at their golf tournament in New Hampshire this summer?" he says. "All the old Bruins show up every year and each year they pick one guy who they feel represented what a Bruin should be. Last year they picked Derek Sanderson and the year before it was Terry O'Reilly. This year [1998] they picked me. They gave me a replica of a Stanley Cup ring. It felt good when Milt Schmidt, a man I'd played with, a man who'd coached me, came across the room and shook my hand. 'Jerry, you really deserved it,' he said. 'I always said you were one of the most honest players I ever worked with.' You're always happy when you receive a little recognition when you're in front of your peers."

"Did you have to make a speech?" I ask.

He laughs. "No way. They know I'm a man of few words. Actually, they knew if they asked me to speak they'd never get me to sit down."

"That ring must mean a lot to you. You never won a Stanley Cup ring, did you?"

"No, but there's an Englishman who may think I did."

"What do you mean?"

"Well, Henri Richard and I were playing golf one day with the president of this big company, a man from London, England. He didn't know that Henri Richard had won eleven Stanley Cups with Montreal. In fact, he didn't know much about hockey at all. On one hole he said to me, 'Jerry, how many Stanley Cup teams did you play on?' And I said to him, 'Well, between Henri Richard and myself, we won eleven.'"

Topper does have a way with words. I remind him I interviewed him on TV at the Boston Garden for CBS back in 1960. I asked the first question and never got to my second. He rambled on about the Bruins for at least three minutes and was still talking when the TV producer frantically began calling for a commercial break. I said before throwing the cue, "Jerry, you are without doubt the easiest player to interview I've ever encountered."

Now, almost forty years after that interview, he tells me a story that's a complete surprise.

"I'm at the NHL meetings in Montreal one summer — it was 1974 — and I don't have a job in hockey. But I'm hoping for something. The Bruins at the time were trying to hire Don Cherry as their new coach. But Cherry was reluctant to move to Boston. He owned 25 percent of the Rochester franchise and he's really popular there, really popular.

"So Lynn Patrick, who was then general manager in St. Louis, calls me. He says, 'Listen, Jerry. It's obvious Cherry is not going to Boston. You'd be ideal for that job. So I spoke to Harry [Sinden] about you. Are you interested in coaching the Bruins?' I said, 'You kidding? Of course I'm interested.'

"So Lynn calls Harry and that day I get word that Harry wants to see me. I meet with Harry and he tells me Cherry isn't taking the job, that he wants me to take it. He tells me not to say a word about the opening and tells me he'll meet me in his office back in Boston three days later — on a Friday. 'We'll work out all the details then,' he says. 'We'll arrange a press conference and you'll be the next coach of the Boston Bruins.'

"Boy, was I happy. Wow! Coach of the Bruins. Thank you very much, Harry.

"That night we go out for some drinks. Don Cherry was in the group and I start telling him how stupid he was not to take the Boston job. Hey, what do I care now that Harry's chosen me for the job. The more we drink the more I tell him what a dummy he is to stay in Rochester.

"I was living in Springfield then and the next morning I'm driving back home with my good friend Walt Atanas. At noon we stop at some roadside joint and go inside for a bite to eat. Over coffee Walt says, 'Jerry, I'm worried about you. No job, no prospects. I wish I could help you land something for the winter.'

Of course I hadn't told Walt about my conversation with Harry. I'd promised not to breathe a word of it. I just grinned and said, 'Walt, don't worry about Topper. I always land on my feet. I'm going to be just fine. You're going to be reading a lot about me in the next few days.'

"I went to order a sandwich when I looked up at the TV set on the wall and there was a sports bulletin. The announcer says, 'Don Cherry has just signed a contract to coach the Boston Bruins.'

"I turned to Walter and I said, 'Walter, on the other hand, I might be able to use all the help I can get this winter.'

"And that's a true story."

When I stop laughing, I ask Jerry if there was a single performance as a Bruin that stands out in his memory.

He grins. "Well, not many people know this but I'm the only player in history to score four goals in a game — one that ended in a 2–2 tie."

"What?"

He begins to laugh. "One night I scored two goals against Montreal and two goals against my own team. The last two were accidental, of course. But that's one helluva record, isn't it?

"Another funny thing happened to me during my final season in hockey," he recalls. "After a game a father approaches me and asks me to sign his son's program. While I'm signing, the kid looks up at me and says, 'How old are you, Mr. Toppazzini?' Well, I was about 35 years old then but I say to the kid, 'Son, how old do you think I am?' He stares up and me and says, 'Forty-five?' I say, 'Son, you're out by ten years.' And he says, 'You mean you're 55?'"

"You're a funny man, Topper."

"Me? You want funny, you should talk to Leo Labine. He had the guys in stitches at the golf tournament."

Labine Was a Mean Little Bugger

J ERRY Toppazzini is talking about his good friend Leo Labine, a Bruin for ten years in the 1950s.

"Leo had the worst shot in hockey. Nevertheless he was all hockey player and a mean little bugger. In my opinion, pound for pound he was the toughest player in hockey in our era. He never skated away from the trouble, he skated right into it. Once you put a stick in Leo's hand, look out. He used to say, 'Only beavers eat lumber and I'm no beaver.'

"I remember our rookie year and the first game we played in Hershey. The game has barely started when Leo gets in a stick fight with Pete Durham of Indianapolis. You couldn't believe the way those sticks were flying. It's a wonder they didn't kill each other. I was at the end of the bench and all I thought about was getting back to Copper Cliff. I wasn't going to stick around if this was the way the pros played the game. It was vicious.

"Leo hit a guy — Jim Enio I think it was — in that game and I think it was the last game Enio ever played. In Detroit one night, Leo went after Gordie Howe, of all people. I couldn't believe it, this bantamweight rookie swinging his stick at big Howe.

"Bill Ezinicki was a tough guy, too, and we played his team in Hershey one night. Ezzy was in the penalty box and Leo skated right up to the box and began snarling at him. 'You may scare some of the guys in this goddamn league but you don't scare me,' he yelled at Ezzy. Before Leo got the last word out, Ezzy's big fist shot out and smashed into Leo's nose. Did he cork him! Blood starts flying out of his nose and his gloves fall off.

"Geez, we've laughed about that incident over the years. It's even funnier when Leo tells that story.

"Another funny thing about Leo. He never seemed to know when we were playing. One time I had to drag him out of a theater because there was a game that night and Leo had forgotten all about it. Grabbed a cheese sandwich on the way to the rink.

"In Buffalo one night, we had to change trains on our way back from Toronto to Boston. Leo got off the train to buy a sandwich and when the train started to move he wasn't on it. He got on the train on the next track by mistake, one heading in the opposite direction. Now the train starts moving and we look out the window and there's Leo on the train across from us — sitting there eating his sandwich. We had to make an emergency stop and wait until he scrambled back on board."

Boivin's Body Checks Earned Him Hall of Fame Berth

LEO Boivin was built like a fire hydrant, and was just as solid. In junior hockey in the late 1940s, first with the Inkerman Rockets and then the Port Arthur West End Bruins, his ability to knock the socks off opposing forwards with devastating checks earned him high praise from the Boston Bruins' management. Bruin fans couldn't wait to see this heralded youngster in action.

But when they finally did, he was no longer Bruin property — he was a member of the hated Toronto Maple Leafs. In 1952–53, the Bruins traded the rookie Boivin, along with Fern Flaman, Ken

Smith, and Phil Maloney, to the Leafs in return for Vic Lynn and Bill Ezinicki.

It didn't take long for the Bruins to realize they had made a huge mistake. So in 1954, they got Boivin back, giving up forward Joe Klukay in the deal. By then Boivin was a polished defender, one who was known league-wide for his crushing body checks. His hip checks alone caused many opponents to believe they'd been sideswiped by a runaway Zamboni.

Boivin's body work helped carry the Bruins to consecutive hard-fought Stanley Cup finals in 1957 and '58.

He served as Boston's team captain until the mid-'60s when he was traded to Detroit for Gary Doak, Bill Lesuk, and future considerations.

His many fans in Boston applauded his induction into the Hockey Hall of Fame in 1986. Now 67, widowed, and living in Prescott, Ontario, Boivin was profiled recently in the *Toronto Star*. He told writer George Gamester his hips are just fine, but his other body parts have been afflicted by arthritis.

"And I still get plenty of requests for autographs," he adds. "Some kids write, 'My dad says you were the hardest hitter in NHL history.'"

The Boston Shadows

D URING the 1953 playoffs, Lynn Patrick, the Bruins' coach, would do whatever it took to win. He would dress different players each night depending on the style of game he wanted to play. If he felt that the Bruins lacked defense, he would sit his best offensive threats for defensive specialists. If he felt that his team wasn't scoring, he would only play his best offensive players.

Before the first game of a series between the Bruins and the Red Wings, Patrick held a meeting for his players. He told his team, "Don't worry, we're going to show them a thing or two. We'll have a few tricks up our sleeves." Patrick's plan was to cover Detroit's best players, Gordie Howe and Ted Lindsay. He figured that if the Bruins could stop those two guys, they could handle the entire Detroit team.

Patrick assigned Boston's best defensive player, Woody Dumart, to check Gordie Howe and do nothing else. Patrick also assigned Joe Klukay, another solid defensive player, to stay on Lindsay for the entire game. What developed out of Patrick's strategy was hockey's first "shadows." Somehow Lindsay and Howe managed to duck their "shadows" and Detroit easily won the first game 7–0.

The Bruins were deflated by the convincing Detroit victory when Patrick called another meeting. "Don't worry, we'll be all right. We just have to make a few adjustments, we'll be ready for the next game." After the meeting, Patrick told Woody to continue to shadow Howe during the game. "If Howe goes to the men's room, you go with him."

The Bruins made the necessary adjustments and stuck to the new game plan. Woody did just as his coach instructed him to, never allowing Howe out of his sight. The Bruins kept up this strategy for the duration of the series and upset Detroit in six games.

After the series, Howe announced he was getting married. When Woody heard the news he smiled and said, "Here I've been so close to Howe during the past two weeks and he didn't even tell me about it!"

The Lindsay–Ezinicki Feud

DETROIT Hall of Famer Ted Lindsay recalls in detail his famous feud with former Bruin Bill Ezinicki:

"Our feud goes back to junior hockey when I played for St.

Mike's in Toronto and he was with the Oshawa Generals. He was the tough guy in the league but I wasn't going to let him run me. I figured he bleeds just like I do. Anyway, when St. Mike's was knocked out in the playoffs in 1944, Oshawa picked me up and I wound up on a Memorial Cup winner, playing on a line with Ezinicki.

"We both turned pro and I played against him many times, first when he was with Toronto and then with the Bruins where he played in the early fifties. We were always at each other's throats.

"One night in Detroit the whistle had gone and we tangled right in front of the Boston bench. Well, he took his stick and hit me right below the hairline and the blood began to flow. I couldn't let him get away with that. If I did, all the fans would think I was scared. So I took my stick and whacked him over the head in about the same place and he started to bleed. He dropped his stick and gloves and came after me. Remember, he was a tough guy and very strong and I had no place to hide. We started throwing punches and I gave him a pretty good beating. I cut him for about 20 stitches and I knocked a couple of his teeth out. But I was relieved when the fight was over.

"But when I turned away and started skating to the penalty box I heard Gordie Howe cry out, 'Look out, Ted! Here he comes!' Ezzie had broken away from the linesmen and was tearing after me. When he moved in, I let him have it with as hard a punch as I've ever thrown and it connected. He fell right down on the seat of his pants and his head flew back and hit the ice. Remember, we didn't wear helmets in those days. Then I straddled him and I was throwing punches when I heard Gordie yell, 'He's out, Ted. He's out.' And I said, 'I don't give a damn. I'm going to kill him.' But they finally hauled me off him and led me away.

"I went to the dressing room and showered and I was told that Ezzie had been taken to the first aid room. When I was dressed I passed by the room and pushed open the door. I said, 'You all right, Ezzie?' He just snarled, 'I'll get you, you son of a bitch.' I backed out and closed the door. Our feud lasted for as long as we played against each other."

Bruin defenseman Murray Henderson was on the Boston bench that night, a witness to the Ezinicki beating.

"If I have one regret about my hockey career, it was that I didn't jump off the bench and go after Lindsay that night," he says. "To this day I don't know why I didn't. It was like we all froze watching Lindsay beat up on Ezinicki. It was brutal. Ezzie was a good bodychecker but he wasn't really a fighter. I know if I'd been on the ice at the time I would have jumped Lindsay. But I was on the bench. And none of us went to Ezzie's aid and we should have. I should have and I didn't."

Lindsay had a final word about playing at the Boston Garden.

"The old Garden was a tough rink to play in for the visiting team. In the stands there were all these loudmouth people and they always got on Gordie (Howe) and me. Gordie especially because he was big and he had some great nights against the Bruins. I remember the long corridor we had to walk from the dressing room to the ice and how the fans would line up on each side to heckle us. Howe and I were always the last out of the room and we learned to hold our sticks close into our bodies with about eight inches of shaft sticking out. We were always wary of something taking a swing at one of us and when they did, we would take a swing back at them. After they tasted the shaft of a hockey stick a couple of times, they learned their lesson and backed off."

5

Orr Comes to Town

A Dreadful Incident

MY friend in broadcasting, the late Dan Kelly, often referred to the 1969 stick-swinging battle between the Bruins' Ted Green and the Blues' Wayne Maki as "one of the most horrifying, most violent exchanges I've ever seen in hockey."

It happened on September 21, 1969, during a preseason game in Ottawa. Kelly was calling the play-by-play for a St. Louis radio station that night. Early in the game, Green and Maki collided in the Boston zone. Linesman Ron Finn, officiating in only his fourth NHL game, was nearby when they bumped, close enough to feel the breeze when Green turned and swung his stick viciously at Maki, missing him by a few inches. Maki retaliated instantly with a stick swing of his own, catching Green flush on his unprotected head. Green dropped to the ice and lay there, barely conscious and groaning.

"I could see right away that Green was badly hurt," Kelly told me fifteen years after the incident. "When he tried to get up, his face was contorted and his legs began to buckle under him. It was dreadful. I almost became physically ill watching him struggle because I knew this was very, very serious. I remember it like it happened yesterday."

Green fell back, unable to help himself. Finn and the other officials, linesman Rob Waddell and referee Ken Bodendistel, waved for the trainer and a doctor. They, too, sensed that Green was in serious trouble. Boston's toughest player was rushed to hospital, where doctors diagnosed a depressed fracture of the skull near the right temple. Five hours of surgery and a follow-up operation were required to save his life.

After the game, the three officials were interviewed by Ottawa police. Assault charges were laid against Green and Maki. Meanwhile, the NHL took disciplinary action, suspending both players and fining each $300. In retrospect, the suspensions appear ludicrous, although a league official called them "the stiffest in league annals." Maki was suspended for thirty days and Green for thirteen games, "if and when he returns to hockey."

The game had not been televised so there were no replays of the incident. And no professional photographs were taken. However, a 12-year-old boy at rinkside snapped a photo at the moment Green was struck. Finn said, "I heard later the kid made enough money off that photo to put himself through college."

Kelly recalled his feelings for Maki. "Some of the Bruins — Orr and Ace Bailey and others — leaped off the bench and attacked Maki, who stood there, looking bewildered and vulnerable. At that moment I really admired Maki because the kid had to stand up for himself. Perhaps he was shocked at what had happened as everybody in the building. You see, Green was such a renowned tough guy. And for this kid to stand up to him was a revelation. I think he stood up to him because he was terrified, like he was trapped in a corner. I certainly wish — and I know Maki wished until the day he died — that he'd never hit Green. But he did hit him, and I remember thinking at the time, well, this kid is in big trouble but he has a lot of guts."

Weeks later, brought to trial, both players were exonerated in an Ottawa courtroom. Green's injury, thought to be career-ending, kept him out of hockey for a year. In 1970–71, with a metal plate in his head, he made a stunning comeback with the Bruins. No longer the league's toughest player, he was, however, a key performer in Boston's run to the Stanley Cup in 1972. He jumped to the WHA a few weeks after the Cup win and played in the rival league for seven more years, retiring in 1979. In the '90s he has served as a head coach and assistant coach with the Edmonton Oilers.

Wayne Maki's NHL career was cut short by a brain tumor, discovered when he was a member of the Vancouver Canucks. He passed away from the cancer in the spring of 1974.

Shortly after the incident, Boston coach Milt Schmidt purchased two dozen helmets and issued them to his players. When he showed up for practice the following day, none of the Bruins was wearing them. He ordered them to don the headgear or get off the ice. The players turned to look at Bobby Orr. Head down, Orr skated slowly off the ice, followed by his teammates.

Schmidt decided not to make an issue of it and the helmets were stored away.

Unbelievable!
A Defenseman Wins
the Scoring Crown

PRIOR to the 1969–70 season, hockey people and fans alike thought it impossible for a defenseman to win the individual scoring title in the NHL. By the end of that season, Boston's multi-talented Bobby Orr had changed their thinking, had changed the face of hockey — and the role of the game's defensemen — forever.

With 120 points, 21 more than teammate Phil Esposito, Orr shattered the long-standing myth that defensemen were supposed to be guardians, not goal scorers. Coaches of the day expected their blueliners to stay at home, to know their place. But Orr was a mold-breaker, a visionary. In the next four years he finished second in the scoring race three times and third once (all four times behind Esposito).

Then, in 1974–75, he zoomed right to the top again. Orr captured his second Art Ross Trophy, finishing with the most points in the regular season with 135. No defenseman has won a scoring title since. Orr's fantastic point production proved that he was a gifted offensive player, and it could be argued his offensive stats overshadowed his defensive skills. How good was he from the blueline to his own net? One of Orr's most amazing stats is his career plus-minus rating. Over his 657-game career, Bobby amassed an amazing rating of plus-597. One season he was better than plus-100. In 1970–71, he was plus 124.

A Heartbreaking Loss for Horvath

ON March 20, 1960, the Bruins and the Blackhawks met at the Garden in the final match of the season. Bruins center Bronco Horvath, playmaker on the prolific Uke Line, had grabbed the hockey spotlight and was on the verge of snaring the Art Ross Trophy as NHL scoring champion. With 60 minutes to play in the regular season, Horvath led Chicago susperstar Bobby Hull by a single point in the race for the Ross.

Horvath, who'd never been in such lofty company before and never would be again, knew it might be his only chance to capture one of the NHL's top prizes. At age 30, he desperately wanted to beat 21-year-old Hull and win that trophy.

But his hopes took a header shortly after the opening faceoff. Midway through the first period, Boston defenseman Bob Armstrong wired a shot from the blueline that hit Bronco squarely in the jaw. Horvath flopped to the ice, unconscious. He was carried off the ice and rushed by ambulance to the hospital. On the way, Horvath recovered sufficiently to begin screaming, "Go back! Go back! I want to play! I want to play!" At the hospital, he refused to take off his uniform or his pads while doctors hovered over him. X-rays were taken and there was a delay while the medics examined the film. They finally concluded that Bronco's jaw was severely bruised, but not broken.

Bronco bolted for the door. He was rushed back to the Garden, where he threw on his skates and played the final few minutes of the third period. By then his slim lead in the scoring race had evaporated. While he was away, Bobby Hull had recorded two points in a 5–5 tie to win his first scoring crown.

A disconsolate Horvath had to settle for the runner-up spot. And he would never challenge again. The following year he slumped to 15 goals and 30 points, 50 points fewer than his banner season. He often wondered what might have been if his teammate hadn't kayoed him in that final game of the 1959–60 season.

A hockey oddity earlier in the 1959–1960 season also contributed to Horvath's loss of the scoring title.

Playing against the Blackhawks on November 8, Horvath was tripped from behind on a breakaway. Referee Dalt McArthur awarded a penalty shot to the Bruins.

In a bizzare interpretation of the rules, McArthur allowed the *Blackhawks* to select a Bruin player to take the shot. Chicago chose a utility player named Larry Leach to take the free shot — and he missed. McArthur should have allowed the Bruins to pick the shooter. Had he done so, Horvath would have been their choice. The missed opportunity may have cost Horvath a tie (with Hull) for the scoring title. McArthur's glaring gaffe cost him his job, for his contract was not renewed.

Swedish Humorist Sent Packing

T HE Boston Bruins were one of the first NHL clubs to sign a hockey player from Sweden. They had high hopes for Sven (Tumba) Johanson, a four-time Olympian, who joined the Bruins at training camp more than thirty years ago. Alas, Johanson's stay in the NHL was a brief one.

"I don't think the Bruins accepted me," he said on his return to Sweden, "and I'm sure it was because of a practical joke I played on them one day. I saw that they all joked around with each other in the dressing room and I liked that. I wanted very much to be a part of it. So I asked myself what I could do to become accepted by them?

"Well, I noticed they all put their false teeth in little cups before a game or practice. So I thought I'd have some fun. When they went on the ice I sneaked back into the room and switched all the teeth around. When they came back in, and tried to slip their dentures in they found that none of them fit. Did they laugh at my little prank? No, were they ever mad! And they knew it was me who'd done it because I was laughing like crazy. Instead of accepting me they completely rejected me.

"From then on it was very cool between us. A few days later the manager took me aside and told me he was sending me back to Sweden. Obviously, the Bruins didn't appreciate my Swedish sense of humor!"

A Night for the Chief

D URING the 1967–68 season the Boston Bruins held a night for one of their most popular players, veteran left winger Johnny Bucyk. Bucyk had played spectacular hockey for the Bruins for the past decade as a member of the Uke Line. Now it appeared he was beginning to lose his touch. His goal production had slipped to 18 the previous season. Perhaps he should consider retirement while he was still on top. Bucyk was given a new car, an outboard motor, and other gifts, as well as much praise for serving the Bruins so well and for so long. At the end of the on-ice ceremony, it seemed that everyone expected Bucyk to announce that he was in his final year of hockey.

But that was never his intention. At the age of 32, Bucyk had no plans to buy a rocking chair, to fish from his new boat, or whack golf balls into the sunset. He came back to the Bruins the following year and recorded a 30-goal season. Then, playing like a kid again, he scored 24, 31, and, incredibly, 51 goals. At the age of 35 he became the only player of that vintage to score 50 or more goals in a season. Nobody since has duplicated the feat.

Even then, Bucyk gave no thought to retirement. Five years after that 51-goal season, he connected for 36 goals. Only when he turned 43, more than a decade after his "Night," did he decide it was time to step aside — after a "disappointing" season in which he scored a mere 20 goals.

Eleven years had passed since he'd been honored on Johnny Bucyk Night. The car and the boat's motor had long since worn out. During those years, Johnny helped the Bruins to a pair of Stanley Cup victories. He'd received several individual honors, including a pair of Lady Byng trophies. He'd scored an incredible 319 goals since his "retirement party" and 556 in all, to become the fourth-leading scorer of all time.

When it comes to durability, the man they called the Chief ranks right up there with Gordie Howe.

A Writer Remembers Orr

RUSS Conway is on the phone from Lawrence, Massachusetts. He's the sportswriter from the *Lawrence Eagle-Tribune* who was nominated for a Pulitzer Prize for his exposé of Alan Eagleson, articles that helped in the conviction of the former executive director of the NHLPA for fraud. Russ is talking about Bobby Orr.

"It was a long time ago, maybe twenty-five years, when Bobby was at the peak of his game, the greatest player in hockey. I was on my way to a Bruins' morning practice and it was one of those days when everything was going wrong in my life. You know how it is, the car wouldn't start, I slipped on a patch of ice, I found some letters I forgot to mail — a dozen little things that really aggravated me. So when I get to the Boston Garden and pass Bobby Orr he slaps me on the shoulder and says, 'Russ, How's everything?'

"I say, 'Everything's horseshit' or something similar, because I'm having a lousy day.

"Bobby laughs and says, 'I've got a cure for that. Meet me after practice.'

"So now I'm curious and of course I meet him after practice.

"'Come with me,' he says. We go into the Bruins' dressing room where I wait while he showers and gets dressed. Then he talks to the trainer and the trainer loads him up with a lot of pucks and sticks and team souvenirs and we go to the parking lot. He throws all this stuff in the trunk of his Cadillac, tells me to hop in and we drive off. He doesn't say a word as we drive away. I have no idea where he's going or what he has in mind.

"Now he pulls off the highway and drives into the parking lot of a major hospital. 'Get out,' he says. Then he turns and wags a finger at me. 'Not a word of this trip gets in your newspaper. A deal?'

"'Sure, Bobby. If you say so. It's a deal.'

"In the hospital he says hello to everyone he meets. The

nurses, the staff, the doctors he passes in the halls. Then he makes his way to the children's ward. Obviously he knows the way because he doesn't need to ask directions. He goes from room to room, from bed to bed. Keep in mind these are sick kids — cancer patients and others with major health problems. But they all know Bobby Orr and how their faces light up when he kibitzes with them and hands out his hockey souvenirs — photos for all, a stick here and a puck there. I get a big lump in my throat watching all this.

"Finally, he says his goodbyes and we turn to go.

"'Not so fast,' says Bobby. 'We've got two more floors to cover.'

"It's another hour before we're out of there. And the lump in my throat has doubled in size by the time we reach the parking lot.

"He starts the Caddie and we drive away, neither of us talking, both of us moved by the experience. Finally he turns to me and grins. He says, 'Well, Russ, how's your day now?'"

Scoring with a Broken Back

FORMER Bruin Dean Prentice is the only NHL player ever to score a goal while playing with a broken back. Prentice, who played in the NHL for twenty-two years and scored 391 goals with five different clubs, was with the Bruins from 1962–63 to 1965–66. One night in Chicago he was tripped from behind while on a breakaway. He went crashing backfirst into the end boards behind the Chicago goal. Knocked cold, he opened his eyes to see a number of players hovering over him. Chicago star Bobby Hull was one of them.

"Dean, you've been given a penalty shot. But you're hurt. You're going to have to let one of the dummies on your team take it."

"Like hell I am, Bobby," Prentice said, now almost fully conscious. He scrambled to his feet and convinced the referee he was ready to take the free shot.

"I grabbed the puck, skated in, gave Glenn Hall a little deke, and drilled it upstairs. Top shelf. The red light flashed. Then I skated to the Boston bench and sat down.

"Two minutes later, the coach signaled me to take a shift. To my consternation, I couldn't move. Couldn't move my legs to get over the boards.

"Somehow, in great pain, I was able to hobble back to the dressing room. And I managed to fly back to Boston with my teammates after the game. Once home, I was taken immediately to hospital and stayed there for the next six weeks. Seems I'd fractured a couple of vertebrae in my back. I wondered if I'd ever be able to play again. Perhaps that penalty shot goal was to be my NHL swan song.

"They operated and put me in a full body cast. That made me even more pessimistic. I remember the embarrassment of going to the bathroom and not even being able to wipe myself. It was mortifying.

"But I made a fine recovery and played for another eight or nine years.

"By the way, you can tell the fans in Boston I really enjoyed my time there. A great franchise, a wonderful city."

I told Dean, "Your name comes up from time to time as a worthy candidate for the Hockey Hall of Fame. Someone who's been overlooked. Does it bother you that many of your former teammates, men like Andy Bathgate, Harry Howell, and Gump Worsley are in the Hall and you're not?"

His answer was straight from the heart. "Yes, it does. I'm proud of my record — twenty-two years and almost 400 goals. But as you know I'm a devout Christian and a great believer that what will be, will be."

Orr Almost Kills Teammate

NO doubt Bobby Orr still shudders when he thinks about it, the day he almost killed Eddie Johnston. It happened back in the late sixties when the Bruins were warming up for a game against the Red Wings at the old Detroit Olympia.

Orr drilled a practice shot at the net and the puck struck Johnston, who didn't wear a mask, on the side of the head, right by the temple.

Johnston dropped like a rock. Orr and the rest of the Bruins raced to the scene and Orr felt ill when he saw his teammate's ashen face. Clearly, the injury was a serious one. The team trainers rushed out and carted Johnston off the ice. An ambulance was called and, its siren screaming, drove Johnston to a nearby hospital.

Doctors found blood clots in the goaltender's head and expressed concern for his survival. His condition was critical. Over the next two days they became more alarmed over their patient's sudden weight loss.

"They figured it was all over for me," Johnston said, reflecting on his brush with death. "Someone called a priest and he stayed with me for the next two weeks. I didn't know about it until later because I was completely out of it. For five weeks I had no idea what was going on.

"My family came to visit and I didn't even recognize them. Couldn't remember names or anything. And the doctors didn't want me to sleep for fear I'd never wake up again. The question wasn't whether I'd play hockey again but whether I'd make it through to the following day.

"Finally, after eight weeks they check my head again and find nothing. I told them that's no big surprise. I told them all goalies are empty-headed. No brains to begin with. They told me my sense of humor was a good sign, that I'd probably make a full recovery."

Johnston did recover and went on to play many more seasons in the NHL. But he'll never forget — and neither will Orr — how a shot fired high in a pregame warmup almost ended his career — and his life.

Keep Your Head Up, Storey

FORMER NHL referee Red Storey loved working games at the Boston Garden. Perhaps because officiating a game there always presented a challenge. The ice surface was the narrowest in the NHL and the team benches were on opposite sides of the rink. That meant a referee had to step lively when teams made line changes. Otherwise he could be bowled over.

Red recalls the days when workmen were handed rifles and ordered to go in and shoot the rats and pigeons that called the Garden home. During games, as the most unpopular man in the building, he often worried that someone might take a shot at him.

One night a cowboy in the balcony tried to snare Red with a hangman's noose. Red was at the boards, following the play, when he heard one of his linesmen shout, "Red, look out!" Red looked up in time to dodge a length of rope that was dangling over his head. And the rope ended in a noose!

"I don't know what the guy had in mind," Red said. "Maybe he hoped to catch me around the neck and string me up. I was used to the fans in Boston throwing stuff — like a metal bolt which just missed my head one night, or the time a ripe tomato struck me on the neck. I thought I'd been shot because my jersey was covered in what looked like blood. Then I realized it was just tomato juice. But a hangman's noose? I'd never encountered anything like that before."

What's the best line Red ever heard from a fan? "That's easy," he says, laughing. "The guy who yelled, 'Hey Storey, you must be pregnant. You've already missed two periods.'"

Kilrea on Shore

BRIAN Kilrea, the highly successful coach of the Ottawa 67's, played for Eddie Shore in Springfield throughout the sixties. Some of his stories about the man border on the unbelievable.

"During one season I was with Shore, we had to travel to Pittsburgh for a Wednesday game, so Shore holds a practice on Tuesday. But somehow he neglects to tell us we were leaving on the bus right after the practice. We show up at the rink for a noon-hour workout and that's when Eddie tells us that we have to be ready to go at 1:30. Well, most of us didn't bring our travel clothes and when we tell Eddie that he says, 'That's too bad. I don't care. We're leaving at 1:30.' So after practice, the guys all fly home to pack a bag and none of us makes it back to the rink on time. When it's 1:30, Eddie says to the bus driver, 'Hey, start your engine. Let's go.'

"The bussie says, 'But, Eddie, there ain't no players on the bus.'

"'I don't care,' says Shore. 'Let's move.'

"So the bus driver and Eddie take off for Pittsburgh. When the players get back to the arena, we discover that our transportation has gone. It's unbelievable. So we huddle together and decide to drive to Pittsburgh in four or five cars and we get there that night. But this is the start of a road trip — four games in five nights — and we're driving our cars all over the place. On that trip we finish up winning three games out of four despite the screwup at the start of it. Now, Eddie, being the generous soul that he is, won't give us any more than a dollar per meal — three dollars a day — during this trip. Even in those days you couldn't find much on any menu for a dollar.

"Well, we get back home after living on junk food but with six big points added to our total. We're dead tired and expect we're going to be rewarded with a bit of a rest. But no, Eddie won't allow that. We check the calendar and see that he's got an early morning practice scheduled for the next day. Well, that was the straw that broke the donkey's back. I went to the media and said to them, 'You want to know about our road trip? Well, Eddie drives off on the bus without us, we win three out of four, play our hearts out, get squat for food, and now we have to crawl out of bed for an eight o'clock practice. I guess that's Eddie's way of saying thanks. What do you think about the old man now?'

"Well, the reporters loved it. They all published stories on what a cheap, demanding guy Shore is. Shore comes into the dressing room the next day and he's fuming. He gets there late because he never likes to get up early, but he wasn't too late to read the papers and he's irate.

"He yells at me, 'You! Kilrea! Did you have anything to do with this article in this morning's paper?'

"And I try to look innocent and say, 'What article, Eddie? I didn't have time to read the paper today.' He said, 'It was you, all right. Now get in the corner of the rink and do stops and starts until I get you to quit.'

"So I'm on the ice by myself for the next two hours doing stops and starts. Geez, I got a pile of snow piled up to my ankles before he calls a halt. And what do I get for all of my hard work? I get demoted to the fourth line that night.

"Here's another of my favourite Shore stories. Billy Collins, remember him? Played about 700 games in the NHL, eventually. Well, Billy gets sent to us from Toronto for some reason. Shore has the club staying in a hotel in Hamilton when Billy arrives. And right in the lobby he has us doing this dance. It's supposed to teach us footwork and balance, I guess. What it really teaches us is how to make total fools of ourselves. Anyway, Eddie is there teaching us this dance and everyone checking in and out of the hotel is standing around watching and smiling. Of course, they all think we're crazy. Now Billy Collins comes to check in. It's a warm day and he's wearing shorts and his mouth drops open when he sees all these hockey players dancing in the lobby. He comes over to me, says 'Hey, Killer! What the hell is going on?'

"I say, 'Hello, Billy, welcome to the club. Did you bring your dancing shoes?'

"And he says 'Listen, Killer, I gotta see Shore.' Not missing a beat I point him in the right direction. So Billy walks over and says hello to Shore.

"Shore looks him up and down and says, 'Who are you again?'

"Collins says, 'I'm Billy Collins, you just traded for me.'

"Eddie sees that Billy is wearing shorts. He bends down to look at his legs and says, 'You're awful bow-legged! You'll never be a hockey player. Go back to Toronto.' Then Eddie turns and walks away.

"Now, Billy's in shock. He doesn't know what to make of Shore. So he comes back over to me and says, 'Well, what do I do now, Killer?'

"And I tell him, 'Billy, the best possible thing for you to do is to go back to Toronto as fast as you can and tell them Shore doesn't want you!' And that's what he did."

Bruins Accused of Racial Slurs

T HE first time Eddie Shack clashed with Larry Zeidel they both wound up in jail. During an exhibition game on October 1, 1958, Shack, then a rambunctious Ranger prospect playing for Springfield, was challenged by Zeidel, a notorious minor-league tough guy, a member of the Hershey Bears. Zeidel came away from the stick-swinging confrontation with ten stitches holding flaps of skin together on his scalp. Both men were ejected from the game.

"He speared me twice and I told him if he did it again I'd conk him good," Shack recalls.

"When he did it again I nailed him right over the head with my stick."

Still fuming and seeking revenge, Zeidel walked from the dressing room and encountered Shack, who was watching the rest of the game at rinkside. A near riot ensued when the two combatants slugged it out in their street clothes, a brawl that ended only when several Hershey policemen intervened and hauled the players off to jail. Shack was charged with creating a disturbance, Zeidel with assaulting a police officer. Both players spent the night in a cell.

In 1958 Shack was embarking on a hockey career that would take him from the Rangers to the Leafs and then, in the summer of 1967, to the Boston Bruins. Larry Zeidel was a career minor-leaguer whose skills had never earned him a permanent berth in the NHL. He thought it was highly unlikely he'd ever have another run-in with Shack.

But the NHL expanded in 1967, from six teams to twelve, and Larry Zeidel, despite his advancing years, sought big-league employment in a most unusual way. He prepared a glossy resumé containing his career highlights and distributed it to all the new clubs. His strategy worked when the Philadelphia Flyers invited the 39-year-old veteran to training camp and signed him to a contract.

Aside from a big-league paycheck, it meant Zeidel would get another chance to confront his old enemy, Eddie Shack.

During the Flyers' initial season, a storm blew the roof off of the Spectrum in Philadelphia. It forced the Flyers to play a number of "home" games in other arenas and one was a late-season match against Boston at Maple Leaf Gardens in Toronto. Eddie Shack was looking forward to the game. He would be returning to the rink of his greatest triumphs. As a member of the Maple Leafs, he had played on four Stanley Cup–winning teams. And he was anxious to play well against the Flyers. "I've got 18 goals and I want to score over 20," he told reporters.

Larry Zeidel wanted to play well, too. And he planned to stay out of trouble because he was one of only four defensemen dressed by the Flyers. Serving time in the penalty box would hurt his injury-plagued team. The last thing he expected was to be become involved in an incident that would create headlines, like the one he would read in a Toronto paper the following day: "A Sickening Night at the Gardens."

And sickening it was.

Both the Flyers and the Bruins seemed to be on edge from the opening faceoff. The Bruins, who'd finished last or second-last for eight years in a row, were on the verge of making the play-offs. They were especially ornery. The fact that Derek Sanderson, their cocky young rookie, had been escorted off the ice with blood streaming down his face after being hit by a puck didn't help matters. This incident seemed to infuriate the Bruins.

Larry Zeidel, one of the few Jewish players ever to perform in the NHL, was playing his usual aggressive game on the Flyer defense. But during the match he appeared to be shaken by taunts coming from the Boston bench. He would later claim that certain Bruins were guilty of uttering anti-Semitic remarks. In his book *Slashing*, Stan Fischler writes, "The Bruins barbed him with stinging epithets. 'We'll see you in a gas chamber, Jew-boy.'"

Then, on that March 7 night in Toronto, came the rekindling of a ten-year-old feud. Zeidel saw Shack moving across the blue-line and went at him.

Shack would say, "I saw him running at me so I let him have a real good shot like this — with my stick." He showed reporters how he had gripped the stick and delivered a cross check. "Then he [Zeidel] comes back at me with his stick — and he hit me pretty good twice."

Spectators, players, and game officials were all stunned by the ferocity of the stick swinging that followed. Slash! Slash! Slash! Shack and Zeidel were determined to whack each other senseless. Blood gushed from a wound to Zeidel's head. Shack forced Zeidel back, landing four solid swipes with his stick. Shack would tell reporters, "I could have hurt the guy more but I broke my stick — broke it right over his head. I didn't want to hit him too hard and have my stick snap. I didn't want to be in there without a stick."

Finally, the linesmen dashed in and wrestled the sticks from the hands of the enraged combatants.

Referee Bruce Hood banished both players from the game with match penalties. Zeidel required several stitches to his bloody head. Today, Shack denies that he was bloodied in the battle but reporters at the game described a three-stitch cut to his noggin.

Both players were fined and drew suspensions, a penalty that angered Shack. "I got sat down for almost two goddamn weeks," he complained. "And I was going so good."

But he came back to score five more goals, winding up with 23.

Afterwards, there were questions regarding the anti-Semitic taunts that the Bruins were accused of hurling at the Philadelphia defenseman. Zeidel pointed out that Shack was not one of the culprits. The Bruins denied all allegations.

One of the linesmen at the game, Matt Pavelich, has often stated that he heard no such comments. But he has a vivid memory of the bloody duel. Pavelich described the Shack-Zeidel confrontation as "one of the most vicious stick attacks I have ever witnessed."

Quinn Nails Orr

ON April 2, 1969, current Maple Leaf coach Pat Quinn became the most reviled man in Massachusetts. At the Boston Garden that night, during a lop-sided quarter-final playoff game between the Leafs and the Bruins (the Bruins won 10–0), Quinn, a rugged Leaf defenseman, did the unthinkable: he injured Bobby Orr. Quinn dropped Bobby Orr to the ice with a shoulder check, giving him whiplash and a concussion, and a quick trip to a nearly hospital. Fortunately, Orr did not suffer a broken neck, as some had suspected at first.

Orr had been rushing out of his own zone with the puck when Quinn barrelled in from the blueline, catching him with one of the most devastating checks Quinn had ever thrown.

"I saw him with his head down and took a run at him," Pat Quinn says of his memorable hit. "Maybe he didn't see me, maybe he had no room to avoid me. I got him with my right shoulder and I followed through. He hit his head when he went down and it turned deathly quiet when he lay there, not moving. But as soon as they got him off the ice it turned to bedlam."

Quinn drew a penalty despite his protests that the hit was a clean one. In the penalty box he became a target for enraged fans, who all wanted a piece of him. The throng surged forward, shaking their fists and spitting at him. Even the policeman in the box lectured him about the hit. Quinn ducked debris, but he couldn't avoid a flying metal change holder (like the ones bus drivers carry). That hurt.

For some reason, the policeman turned and grabbed Quinn in his arms, perhaps to protect him from the fans. But Quinn wrestled free and accidentally broke a pane of glass with his stick. Another cop was cut by flying glass. Eventually, police escorted Quinn from the penalty box to the safety of the Leaf dressing room. Courageously, he came back to play in the final period despite a barrage of missiles that rained down on him from the crowd.

It took several years before Quinn and Orr agreed to put the incident behind them. They are now good friends.

Orr said recently, "I can't believe it's been thirty years since that happened. Now Pat's one of my favorite guys in hockey."

The Big Bad Bruins

Plimpton in Goal

IN the fall of 1977, George Plimpton, the noted American journalist and sports fan, approached the Boston Bruins with an unusual request. Could he play goal for them in a big-league hockey game? Plimpton thought that if he actually stood between the pipes with fifty pounds of goalie equipment weighing him down, while facing 100-mile-an-hour slapshots, he could write a realistic story on the hazards of goaltending in the NHL.

Bruins coach Don Cherry was not about to let Plimpton suit up for a real game — one that counted — but he would allow the author to represent the Bruins in a brief five-minute trial during a preseason game. And good luck to him. First, Plimpton was required to sign a "no-fault" contract, releasing the Bruins and the NHL from any responsibility for any injuries he might suffer, including death.

Plimpton attended the Bruins' fall training camp and roomed with minor-league goalie Jim Pettie, who instructed him on the fundamentals of netminding.

Cherry couldn't have picked a tougher opponent for his novice netminder than the hard-hitting, fast-skating Philadelphia Flyers. Plimpton would start in a road game at the Spectrum. In the Boston dressing room prior to the author's NHL debut, Gerry Cheevers, Boston's first-string goaltender, gave Plimpton some last-minute advice. "Stand up! Stand up!" he said, referring to the style in which Plimpton was to goaltend. Plimpton misunderstood and thought Cheevers was commanding him to stand up in the dressing room. Plimpton leaped to his feet while the other players in the dressing room chuckled at his gaffe. "Not in here, George, out on the ice," Cheevers said, shaking his head. He turn turned to a teammate and muttered, 'What a basket case this guy is."

During the opening two minutes of the game, Plimpton was perfect. The Bruins went on the attack and kept the puck in the Flyers' zone. Then the tide turned and a wave of Flyers surged into the Boston zone while Plimpton had only a fleeting glimpse of "that awful black puck, sailing elusively between sticks and skates, as shifty as a rat in the hedgerow."

The first shot unleashed by the Flyers found the back of the Boston net, a rocket from the point tipped in by Orest Kindrachuk. Plimpton smacked the side of his helmet with his blocker as Flyers fans laughed at his plight.

After Boston's Bobby Schmautz took a penalty, Plimpton found himself facing the vaunted Flyer power play. One shot flew high and rang off the crossbar. Another screamed by the far corner as Plimpton sprawled awkwardly on the ice. In an effort to get back on his feet, he hugged a defenseman's leg and hauled himself upright. Six Flyer shots were then fired at his net. Incredibly, none went in. One bounced off his mask. The rest hit various parts of his body.

Later, when Plimpton wrote about his goaltending experience in *Sports Illustrated*, he said he could take no credit for any of the saves. "I was," he said, "somewhat akin to a tree in the line of flight of a golf ball."

With the writer's five-minute stint nearly over, Boston's Mike Milbury threw a stick at an incoming Flyer forward. Penalty shot to Philadelphia! The man skating out to take it was none other than former 61–goal scorer Reg Leach. George, you're in deep doo-doo now, Plimpton must have told himself. Leach raced in from center ice while Plimpton, recalling Pettie's advice, moved out to cut down the shooting angle. Leach saw an opening and pulled the trigger, aiming for the bottom corner. Just as Leach released the shot, Plimpton collapsed like a house of cards. Eyes closed and fingers crossed, Plimpton felt the shot tip his skate blade and deflect high into the crowd. The Bruins leaped off the bench and hauled Plimpton to his feet. They dragged him to the Boston bench and tossed him over the boards. "They handled me like a sack of potatoes," he would write. "Do you realize

Leach never played well after that game?" Plimpton observed. "Having me stop that shot of his must have been a terrible shock to him."

He regrets missing a major donnybrook that followed his brief stint in goal.

"I was in the Bruins dressing room having a beer and telling some reporters about the joys and hazards of goaltending. I had no idea a fight had broken out between Wayne Cashman and Paul Holmgren and soon all the players were in it. There was even a battle going on under the stands. And when the Bruins trooped into the room they glared at me, wanting to know where the hell I'd been. Was I part of the team or wasn't I?

"I loved the bond I witnessed among hockey players, the sense of camaraderie. When they go out, they go out together. They love to sit around and tell stories. Why, you could silence a table by telling a Bobby Orr anecdote.

"I was told the Bruins, like all hockey players, would not be intelligent. That's nonsense. There were more books being read at the Boston training camp than any other I attended. They played backgammon and bridge. And the level of humor was very high, relative to other sports."

Plimpton found himself a victim of the Bruins humor when he began to get dressed after his memorable performance. His tie was cut into pieces, the toes had been snipped from his socks and the seat was missing from his underwear. Surprised, he looked to Don Cherry for sympathy.

"Consider yourself lucky, George," Cherry advised. "You've still got your hair, haven't you? That's usually the first thing to go."

Don's Favorite Puckstopper

YOU'RE the coach. It's the seventh game of the Stanley Cup finals. You can have your choice of goaltenders. Who would you pick?

Former Boston coach Don Cherry, now a popular, outspoken commentator on *Hockey Night in Canada*, doesn't hesitate to make his choice. "Just give me Gerry Cheevers," he says. "No question. Cheevers was the best I've seen with the big game on the line."

You might expect Cherry's choice to be controversial. Cheevers didn't fashion a minuscule goals-against average in the playoffs. It was 2.69. And while his postseason record of 53 wins, 35 losses, and 8 shutouts is impressive, it hardly puts him on a par with great playoff performers like Jacques Plante (71–37, 2.16), or Turk Broda (60–39, 1.98).

But when it came to making the big save at the right time, Cherry says Cheevers was the man, a coach's dream. "The guy was terrific," said Cherry, sticking a meaty thumb in the air. "Remember 1971–72? The guy played in 33 consecutive games without a loss. It's still a record."

Anything negative to say about the guy? Cherry is asked.

"No, nothin'. Wait, there is. Terrible in practice, just terrible. He was the worst practice goalie I ever saw. When I was coaching in Boston I often sent him off the ice. Told him to go back in the dressing room and read the *Racing Form* because he was ruining our practices."

Cheevers played on two Stanley Cup–winning teams with Boston, in 1970 and 1972. In thirteen NHL seasons he won 230 games, lost 102, and tied 74. He collected 26 shutouts. He finished his playing career with the Bruins in 1980 and later coached the Bruins for close to five full seasons.

Cheevers' Mask

LONG after he retired from hockey, Gerry Cheevers finally revealed the true story behind the stitches painted on his mask.

"Everybody knows how much I hated practices," he said. "So one day I got hit on the mask by a shot that wouldn't break an egg. I fell to the ice and faked an injury and the trainer ran out and hauled me to my feet and led me off to the dressing room. I was sitting in the room jawing with the trainer and having a soda when Harry Sinden walked in. 'Cheevers, you're not hurt,' he said. 'Get back out there!'

"The other Bruins were all laughing because Harry had caught on to my little ploy, so I figured I'd give them something else to laugh at. I told the trainer to paint a 30-stitch gash on my mask. Then I went out and skated up to Harry. 'You don't think I was hurt? You think I was faking? Well, look at this!' I told him, pointing at the mask.

"It wasn't long before I had the damn mask covered with stitches. People were fascinated with that mask. For some of them, it's the only thing they remember me for."

Espo Almost Missed Out

IT'S difficult to believe that one of hockey's greatest scorers was such a late bloomer. Phil Esposito, with over 700 career goals in the NHL, was 19 years old before he caught on with a Junior A club. Espo, who led all NHL scorers on five occasions, almost got shuffled into the discard file as a teenager. In that era of six NHL clubs, all gobbling up a steady stream of talented kids from Junior hockey, Esposito's name produced a number of shrugs.

As an 18-year-old, he failed a tryout with the Chicago Blackhawks' Junior A club in St. Catharines, Ontario. He was told to drive a few miles down the road to Niagara Falls. Maybe there'd be room for him on that team, he was told.

Niagara Falls manager Hap Emms took one look at the gangly youngster lumbering around the ice and said, "Kid, if you can't make it with St. Catharines, we don't want you here."

"Hap could see that I was a terrible skater," Esposito recalls. "Geez, my brother Tony was a better skater than I was and he was a goalie."

The dejected centerman finally caught on with a Junior B team in Sarnia — for $15 per week. It's a wonder his big-league dreams weren't squashed then and there. Only one or two rookies made the leap to NHL clubs each season and the competition for the handful of jobs was fierce. Junior B grads? They weren't even considered.

Espo's skating improved in Sarnia and he finished second in the scoring race to a future NHL player and coach — Terry Crisp.

His performance earned him another chance with St. Catharines the following season. But the critics were still around and the jibes didn't stop.

"Hey, Fatso!" were among the first words he heard from coach Rudy Pilous in training camp. "Lose twenty pounds and I'll keep you around."

Espo lost the weight and gained a spot on the roster. Then he broke his arm and missed a huge part of the season.

He began his professional career in Syracuse, sometimes playing before fifty people. When the franchise was transferred to St. Louis he still couldn't shake the feeling that he'd been branded a bush leaguer and would probably remain one for the rest of his career.

Despite his misgivings, in St. Louis he ran up 90 points in the 1962–63 season. The parent Chicago Blackhawks called him up the following season, took a look, and sent him back to St. Louis for further seasoning. But when he scored 80 points in 43 minor-league games, they gave him a second chance.

Espo was shocked when he discovered how miserly the Hawks were when it came to wages. "Their offer was so low I almost quit the game," he says. "I knew I could make as much driving a truck back home in the Soo."

Still, the game was fun — more fun than driving a truck — so he decided to stay with it. He turned in seasons of 23, 27, and 21 goals and threw passes onto the stick of a kid named Bobby Hull who converted those passes into 39-, and 52-, and 54-goal seasons.

Espo began to feel he'd become a fixture in Chicago. He began to feel appreciated, especially when he talked management into laying out considerably more money for his services.

Then, during the summer of 1967, after recording a career high for points (61), he was shocked to hear that he'd been traded to Boston. "Geez, it was the last place I wanted to go," he says. "The Bruins were awful — always in last place. They were tailenders for six of the last seven years and second-last the other year.

"And the Hawks showed no class in announcing the deal. They left it up to Don Murphy, the publicity guy, to tell me. He never did get to me so he left a message with my wife. I made sure the folks in Sault Ste. Marie knew all abut it. I went on the radio myself and said, 'Hi folks. Here's a hockey scoop for you. Phil Esposito has just been traded to Boston, along with Ken Hodge and Freddie Stanfield. In return, the Hawks will get Gilles Marotte, Pit Martin, and goalie Jack Norris. This is no hoax.'"

Later, still angry with the Hawks, he left for Boston, determined to turn that moribund hockey team into a winner. And with the help of Hodge and Stanfield, Bobby Orr and Johnny Bucyk, that's exactly what he did.

Today, more than three decades later, whenever people discuss the most lopsided deals in NHL history, the Esposito-to-Boston trade is at or near the top of the list. The verdict is always the same — big advantage to Boston.

Another Huge Deal

PHIL Esposito enjoyed his greatest years in hockey as a Boston Bruin. On March 2, 1969, he became the first player in NHL history to reach 100 points in a season. In 1970 he helped the Bruins win their first Stanley Cup in 29 years. The following year he smashed Bobby Hull's single season goal record (58) with 76 in 78 games. He added 76 assists for a record 152 points, a total unsurpassed until Wayne Gretzky scored 164 points in 1980–81. In 1972, after helping the Bruins to a second Stanley Cup, he led Team Canada to an incredible come-from-behind victory over the Soviet Union in eight games. He led the NHL in scoring five times.

Twelve games into the 1975–76 season, with the Bruins in Vancouver, he was gone. In what reporters always refer to as a blockbuster deal, Esposito and Carol Vadnais were dealt to the New York Rangers for Jean Ratelle, Brad Park, and a fringe player named Joe Zanussi. Esposito was devastated by the trade and so were the Boston players. His mates trashed a hotel room in Vancouver, and later paid thousands in damages. They almost mutinied the following day at practice, reacting sluggishly whenever coach Don Cherry blew his whistle. Finally, Cherry called them together and told them they would be gone too if they didn't follow orders. That got them moving.

Esposito, still in shock, told Cherry, "Geez, Grapes, anywhere but bleepin' New York. I hate the place." Years later, he would confess that the Big Apple had been the ideal destination for him.

Park and Ratelle moved into the Bruins lineup and quickly won over the fans with their stellar play. Cherry loved Ratelle's quiet leadership and has always maintained it was a crime that Park didn't win a Norris or two.

"I held him back, told him not to rush so often, and he said, 'No problem,'" says Cherry. "It probably cost him the Norris because the voters always go for the guys with offensive stats, like 20 or 30 goals."

At first, Harry Sinden was crucified by the sports writers for making the deal. But a Boston turnaround silenced his critics. The club moved from last place to first and stayed at the top for the next four seasons.

Tough Ticket to a Meaningless Game

I T was only an exhibition game played between a touring Soviet team and the Boston Bruins on January 9, 1979. Yet it was tougher to find a ticket to the event than any game in Bruin history. Why? Because it was Bobby Orr Night at the Boston Garden.

The fans turned out to shower all their affection on the man who had ruled the ice lanes at the Garden for more than a decade, a man who had played his position like no one had ever played it before.

Those thirty minutes prior to the opening faceoff were packed with emotion. When Bobby was introduced and he stepped on the ice, head down, wearing a new pinstripe suit, the fans screamed a welcome.

"Baw-bee, Baw-bee, Baw-bee!"

With his wife Peggy by his side, Bobby ginned and waved up at the fans who adored him. For five, seven, ten minutes the ovation went on. Several more minutes passed and the din continued.

It gave those of us involved in the *Hockey Night in Canada* telecast time to reflect on the career of this genuine superstar.

- How he was "discovered" at a Bantam hockey tournament in Gananoque, Ontario, a tiny kid from Parry Sound who caught the eye of a couple of Bruin scouts and soon became Boston property.

- How, as a 14-year-old, he played top-level Junior A hockey with the Oshawa Generals and began smashing records. He was the most publicized Junior player since Jean Beliveau.
- How he was ready for NHL play at age 18, a shoo-in for the Calder Trophy as rookie of the year. The Boston franchise, buried in the basement for years, took on new life with the young phenom as its leader. When it was suggested that Orr wasn't quite as good as contemporaries Gordie Howe and Bobby Hull, Harry Sinden stated, "Howe could do everything but not at top speed. Hull went at top speed but couldn't do everything. Well, Bobby could do everything and do it at top speed."
- In 1969–70, Orr led the NHL in scoring with 120 points, 21 more than teammate Phil Esposito. For a defenseman to win the scoring title was unheard of — a feat unparalleled in the history of hockey. He subsequently finished second in scoring three times and then jumped to the top again in 1974–75 with 135 points.
- As a rookie in 1966–67 he made the Second All-Star Team. From 1967–68 to 1974–75 he was a first-team All Star — eight straight seasons!
- He captured the Norris Trophy as the league's top defenseman eight times — from 1967–68 to 1974–75. He won the Hart Trophy as league MVP three times.
- Until Bobby came along, only one defenseman, Flash Hollett, had ever scored 20 goals in a season. Orr scored 21 in this third season, then 33, 37 twice, and a career-high 46 in 1974–75. (In 1985–86, Paul Coffey broke Orr's record, scoring 48 goals.)
- Knee problems kept him out of the historic Team Canada–Soviet Union series in 1972 but he returned in 1976 to lead Canada to a victory over Czechoslovakia in the first Canada Cup tournament. He was named tournament MVP.
- In 1976, his agent, Alan Eagleson, convinced him to leave Boston (a huge mistake) and wind up his career with

Chicago. But six knee operations had taken their toll and he played in only a handful of games over the next two seasons. He retired from hockey on November 8, 1978.

The ovation at the Boston Garden rolled on and on. Almost half an hour passed before it subsided. Johnny Bucyk, a former Bruins' captain and one of Bobby's teammates for most of his career, stepped on the ice. He unfolded a Boston jersey with Number 4 on the back and presented it to Orr.

"Put it on, put it on!" screamed the crowd.

Bobby grinned and took off his suitcoat. He slipped the jersey over his head to a great roar of approval.

Then came the banner-raising. Bobby's name and number, and the years spanning his brilliant career were printed on the banner. People watched spellbound as it was raised high into the rafters.

Bobby's thank-you speech was brief. It was difficult to hear his words over the roar of the crowd. When it was over, there was another prolonged ovation.

Bobby turned to shake hands with a number of people, including Senator Edward Kennedy, who was in a seat behind the Boston bench.

He waved once more and was gone.

Later it was learned that Orr had consented to the tribute only if any money raised went to charity. More than $18,000 was divided among his four favorite causes — multiple sclerosis, cystic fibrosis, the Boston Children's Hospital, and a private fund for research into a rare brain disease that took the life of a close friend's daughter.

Robert Crane, the Massachusetts state treasurer, said, "People have no idea how many hundreds of hours Bobby has donated to charity in the city's hospitals. How many times he's visited patients in those hospitals. He never sought any publicity for the charitable things he did. The people of Boston loved him as a great athlete and the definitive team player. But their love goes well beyond that. He's a very special person in our hearts."

Reverend Frank Chase, a Boston priest said, "The world is full of little people — like myself. We need our heroes and our superstars to whom we can look for inspiration. It is not easy to be a superstar — to remember the good that an autograph or a hand-shake can do. Bobby Orr does these things all the time."

The coach of the Bruins on Bobby Orr Night was Don Cherry. In years to come, he would fill many of his popular Coach's Corner television segments with lavish praise for Orr. On this night he said simply, "There'll never be another like him."

Fifteen years after Bobby Orr Night, I was invited to play in one of those celebrity golf tournaments with four other golfers. Thanks to the greatest of luck, our celebrity was Bobby Orr. After one or two holes, Bobby was kibitzing with the rest of us like we'd been lifelong pals.

"Good shot! Good shot!" he praised us after any drive that hit the fairway.

"Come on, Bud, we need this putt," he encouraged us on the green.

We finished the round, Orr shook hands with all of us, thanked us for making his day so enjoyable, then limped off on legs that obviously gave him pain.

We gathered in a tight group on the green and watched him go. Then the oldest member of the group found words we all endorsed.

"That's the best day of golf I've ever had," he said. "And all because of the company — because of Bobby Orr. He's the greatest."

With Reece in the Crease . . .

THE Boston Bruins unveiled a new goaltender for the opening game of the 1975–76 season. Dave Reece, who grew up in Troy, New York, a college player at the University of Vermont, had played so well in preseason games that he earned the opening-night assignment against the Montreal Canadiens. It was a huge challenge for the political science grad whose only pro experience was with the Boston Braves and Rochester Americans in the American league. But coach Don Cherry thought he was ready for NHL play and so did the Boston fans. They raised a huge banner at the Garden which read, "With Reece in the Crease, Scoring Will Cease."

The Canadiens, with shooters like Guy Lafleur, Steve Shutt, Jacques Lemaire, and Yvan Cournoyer on the roster, were Stanley Cup–bound that season. They showed no mercy on rookie Reece on opening night, firing seven goals past him before Cherry yanked him from the game.

But Reece was not discouraged. The rookie was eager for another chance. He put the opening-night disaster behind him and performed well in his next dozen starts, allowing only 25 goals and compiling two shutouts. Cherry was pleased and Bobby Orr said, "I like this kid. He's got a lot of talent."

Early in February 1976, the Bruins received good news. Veteran goaltender Gerry Cheevers, who'd played on the 1970 and 1972 Stanley Cup teams for Boston before jumping to Cleveland of the World Hockey Association, announced he was returning to Boston. He joined the Bruins for a game in Toronto on February 7. "He won't be my starting goalie, though," Cherry stated. "He's not in game shape. So it'll be Reece in goal against the Leafs." None of the fans who attended the game, and none of us who were there as part of the *Hockey Night in Canada* telecast crew, will ever forget it. Reece suffered through 60 minutes of torture as Leaf captain Darryl Sittler went on a scoring spree unlike any other in league history. He scored 6 goals and added 4 assists for a 10-point night. It's a record that has never been bettered. Unfortunately for Reece, it marked the last time he would ever be seen in the NHL.

"Darryl was pure magic that night," Reece would say later. "During the game, I didn't realize he was doing all that scoring and going for a record. I was too busy. Sometimes I wonder why Don Cherry didn't pull me after the first five or six goals. Grapes must have had his reasons. I can't blame Cheevers if he didn't want to go into a game like that."

Two days later, Reece was back in the American league, never to return. By the end of 1976–77, he was done for good.

Ten years after the Toronto debacle, his friends held a roast for Reece. They called it "A Night to Disremember," and they screened a tape of all eleven goals scored on him.

After his pro career, Reece returned to Trinity-Pawling, the private school in Pawling, New York, he had attended as a youth. He accepted a dual role there as dean of admissions and hockey coach.

"The students know all about that game in Toronto," he says, "and how I helped Sittler set the record that night. And how I messed up in front of a couple of million people watching on television."

For years after his 10-point night, Sittler would tell banquet audiences the following fib: "Poor Dave felt so miserable after letting in all those goals that night that he decided to end it all. So he went down into the Toronto subway and threw himself in front of a speeding train. And you know what? The train went right through his legs."

Cheevers would say, "I did everything but hide under the Boston bench that night. I was afraid Cherry was going to send me in. I covered my head with a towel and tried to shrink into the ground. If ever there was a game I didn't want to play in, that was it."

Sinden Walks Away

C AN you imagine a winning coach walking away from his job after experiencing the thrill of a Stanley Cup victory?

Harry Sinden did — in 1970.

At age 37, after leading the Bruins from last place to first in a four-year span, after molding one of the highest-scoring teams ever assembled, a team that promised to dominate the game of hockey for the next half dozen seasons, Sinden announced that he was quitting.

The reason was money — the trifling sum of $5,000.

Halfway through the 1969–70 season, Sinden went to team executive Milt Schmidt and asked to discuss his contract for the following season.

"Milt, you know I'm on the second year of a two-year contract," he said. "The Bruins have become a real power in the NHL. Before I came along, they missed the playoffs for seven straight years. I think I deserve a raise for next season."

"How much and for how long?" Schmidt replied.

"The term isn't important — a one-year deal is all right with me. But I'd like a raise of $8,000."

"Wow! That's a lot of money," Schmidt replied. "Too much for me to approve. I'll have to ask Westy (Weston Adams, Jr., then the 26-year-old president of the hockey club). Two days later, Schmidt told Sinden the $8,000 figure was out of the question. Would he take $3,000?

"Is that it?" Sinden said. "Is that all I'm worth to the Bruins?"

"Westy said that's as high as we can go."

Sinden turned and walked out of Schmidt's office, aware that his days as the Bruins' coach were numbered — even if the team went on to win the Stanley Cup.

Two days later Sinden called an old friend, David Stirling, owner of the Stirling-Homex Corporation of Rochester, New York.

"Dave, you offered me an off-season job recently," Sinden reminded him. "I'm ready to get out of the hockey business. You still interested?"

"Harry, we'll take you on full-time whenever you're ready. How about after the playoffs?"

"Sounds good to me."

Sterling understood why Sinden was bitter about hockey — and the Bruins. Aside from his meagre salary, Sinden had not been consulted when the Bruins made a blockbuster deal with Chicago months earlier — acquiring Esposito, Fred Stanfield, and Ken Hodge from the Hawks.

"I was hurt and embarrassed," he told a reporter. "Since I would be coaching the new players, you'd think I'd have been consulted about the deal."

Sinden had other grievances. He and general manager Hap Emms had clashed repeatedly about how to run a hockey team. Emms was a strict disciplinarian whose experience was in Junior hockey, dealing with teenagers. Sinden believed that a coach set the guidelines but lets his athletes play the game. And if his players enjoyed a couple of beers after a hard game, where's the harm?

Another bone of contention: when Sinden fined his players for an offense, he discovered that the fine was often meaningless; management failed to deduct the amount from the player's paycheck. This made the coach look weak and foolish in the eyes of the players.

When the Bruins routed the St. Louis Blues in four straight games in 1970 to capture their first Stanley Cup in twenty-nine years, Harry Sinden was elated. He savored the victory, the parties, and the parade.

Three days later, he told management he would not be back. After twenty years in the game, after winning a world championship as a player (with the 1958 Whitby Dunlops) and a Stanley Cup as a coach, he was going into business with his friend Dave Stirling in Rochester.

And what did the Bruins say?

"Good luck, Harry. We certainly won't stand in your way."

Two years later, disenchanted with the business world, Sinden returned to hockey in a job that appeared to be much cushier than it turned out to be. He was asked to coach Team Canada in what would become known as the "Series of the Century" — an eight-game confrontation with the best players in the Soviet Union. In recording one of Canada's supreme sporting triumphs, Sinden's team overcame a 1–3–1 series deficit by taking three straight one-goal victories in Moscow behind the timely goal scoring of Paul Henderson and the brilliant leadership of Phil Esposito.

Immediately following the 1972 series, Sinden, who missed the 1972 Stanley Cup triumph but made his name on the global stage, returned to his beloved Bruins. Recently he completed his tenth season as president and his twenty-seventh as general manager.

On October 17, 1995, he became the first general manager in NHL history to record 1,000 victories. His teams have captured ten division titles and have combined for 27 winning seasons.

On March 30, 1999, Harry Sinden, who has served the Bruins well for 30 seasons, received the prestigious Lester Patrick Award for outstanding service to hockey in the United States. It completed a hat trick of honors for the popular Sinden. He was elected to the Hockey Hall of Fame in 1983 and the International Ice Hockey Federation Hall of Fame in 1997.

Three Holes for Forty Grand!

PRIOR to one season during the 1970s, Boston goaltender Ed Johnston decided to seek a raise. He went to see Bruins executive vice president Charles Mulcahy and insisted on a pay hike of

$20,000. Mulcahy flatly refused. He said he didn't feel that Johnston was worth that kind of money. Johnston insisted he was.

The two men argued back and forth and when they failed to reach an agreement, Mulcahy, who was a noted golfer, came up with a suggestion. He challenged Johnston to a golf match — three holes of play. If Johnston won, he'd get his boost in salary. The odds appeared to be in Mulcahy's favor because not only had he won several golf tournaments but he had even represented the United States internationally at one point in his career.

Johnston wasn't impressed, even though he was well aware of his boss's reputation on the links. He threw out a counterproposal. "Let's make it double or nothing. If I win, you boost my salary by $40,000 next year. If I lose, there will be no raise."

Mulcahy laughed. "Eddie, you're on. See you on the first tee."

On the day of the match, Johnston's drives were long and straight, his putting deadly accurate. He crushed his boss over the three holes they played. Only after Mulcahy paid up did he find out why Johnston was so eager to gamble his paycheck on three holes of golf. Mulcahy learned that Johnston was one of the finest and most talented golfers ever to play professional hockey.

Later in his career, Johnston became a successful manager, first with the Pittsburgh Penguins, then with the Hartford Whalers. In Pittsburgh, he signed Mario Lemieux to one of the richest contracts in National Hockey League history. But Johnston was smart enough not to get involved in any double-or-nothing golfing gambles with his prize rookie. He knew that Lemieux's golfing skills were awesome, far superior to his own. The subject never came up.

Goodrich Gets a Shot

FOR thirty seconds one day, Dave Goodrich lived out every Bruins fan's dream — a tryout with the National Hockey League team.

The 22-year-old defenseman had been playing hockey since he was eleven. He had even caught on with an intramural team at the University of Massachusetts. He'd never been scouted or invited to a training camp, but that didn't deter him. If the Bruins hadn't heard of him, if they weren't aware of his skills, he'd simply have to show them. So one fall day he hitchhiked to Fitchburg, Massachusetts, and ran eight miles to the Bruins motel in Leominster. There he introduced himself to some Boston officials and asked for a shot at making the team.

Handed the usual "don't call us, we'll call you" line by the Bruins, Goodrich resorted to desperate measures. He sneaked into the team's training camp at the Wallace Civic Center, slipped on his skates in the penalty box, and darted onto the ice.

"What the hell are you doing out here?" asked managing director Harry Sinden, a bit surprised that his training camp roster had increased by one — an awkward skater whose name he didn't know.

"I'm here to try out for your team," Goodrich said eagerly.

"Oh, yeah. Well, I don't want the ice all marked up," Sinden growled.

"I'm really determined to do this," said Goodrich.

Sinden sighed and said, "Okay, let's see what you can do."

Goodrich wheeled around the rink, his skates marking up the ice. About halfway around the oval, he caught an edge and crashed heavily into the boards. He grinned, picked himself up, and confidently skated backwards the rest of the way. He stopped and looked at Sinden for an appraisal.

"That'll be enough," commented Sinden. "Thanks for coming."

Goodrich retrieved his shoes from the penalty box and exited the arena sadly. Asked how it felt to travel so far for such a short trial, he said, "I wanted a tryout with the Bruins and I got one. Sure, it was only thirty seconds, but I'm satisfied with that."

Ross Brooks: The 36-Year-Old Rookie Goalie

IT was a dying dream and Ross Brooks knew it. For thirteen seasons Brooks had played in hockey's minor leagues and was positive he wasn't ever going to play in the National Hockey League. Brooks was 33 years old and had spent the past seven years as a backup goalie with Providence. He was beginning to accept the fact that he was going to play out the rest of his career with Providence when, midway through the 1970–71 season, Brooks received what every player dreads — his outright release.

"I was stunned," he said. "I thought about buying a lunch bucket and finding a job but I still wanted to play hockey more than anything. My wife and I decided to sit down and write a letter to every general manager in every league. It cost us about eight bucks for paper and stamps and the message was simple: I was out of work and wanted to play. Was anybody interested?

"Talk about luck. My letter reached Milt Schmidt of the Bruins just when he was seeking a goalie. He called me and signed me and sent me to Oklahoma City. Then it was on to the Boston Braves (a Bruin farm team in the American league), where I shared goalie-of-the-year honors with Dan Bouchard. When Bouchard was drafted by Atlanta, an expansion team, and when Gerry Cheevers went to the WHA, I got a call from the Bruins and finally found myself in the NHL. I was 36, one of the oldest rookies ever, and while it was no big deal, I became one of a small number of Jewish goaltenders ever to play in the NHL (others included Washington's Bernie Wolfe and Chicago's Mike Veisor)."

Getting to the NHL was a total surprise to Brooks and he was determined to make the most of his opportunity. For the next three seasons he played the best hockey of his career. During one stretch he won fourteen consecutive games to equal a team mark set by legendary Bruin goaltender Tiny Thompson in 1929–30.

By the end of his first season, Brooks had compiled an incredible record of 11–1–3 with a goals-against average of 2.64. For the next two seasons, playing backup to Gilles Gilbert, Brooks was always ready and reliable. He retired in 1974 with an extraordinary major-league record of 37 wins, 7 losses, and 6 ties. Brooks' career goals against average was a minuscule 2.64 — lower than that of two Bruin Hall of Famers, Gerry Cheevers (2.84) and Frankie Brimsek (2.70).

"A lot of people, especially young people, could look at my story and learn something from it," Brooks said after he departed the scene with no regrets. "After so many years of people not knowing I was alive out there, after a lot of perseverance and hard work, I finally achieved my goal and proved myself with the greatest team in hockey."

A Legend Turns Fifty

NO book on the Bruins would be complete without several hundred words about Bobby Orr, the greatest Bruin of them all.

Recently, Bob McKenzie, associate editor of *The Hockey News*, filled almost two full pages in his popular publication with a firsthand account of the hockey legend who had just turned 50.

On the occasion of his fiftieth birthday, Bobby Orr did what he does most days.

He got up at 5 a.m.

"I've never been much of a sleeper, even when I played," Orr said during an early-morning birthday interview with *The Hockey News*. "The truth is I can't sleep too long. No matter what time I go to bed, no matter how late it is, I don't sleep more than five hours. I wake up a lot, which is fine because this is the best part of the day anyway."

On this particular day, Orr was at his secondary residence in Jupiter, Florida. It would be a misnomer to call it a vacation home, especially now that the Hall of Fame defenseman has immersed himself in the sports agent business as one of the owners and hardest-working employees of Bob Woolf and Associates, the Boston-based representation firm. While he had an 8 a.m. tee-off time planned with former Boston Bruins mate Gary Doak — call it a birthday present to himself — Orr was coming off a busy couple of days of servicing clients.

Orr had spent time with St. Louis Cardinals pitcher Matt Morris. Then it was off to Orlando to meet with Eric Nickulus, an unsigned Bruins draft choice who's playing in the International league. Orr was in Orlando for a couple of days and didn't arrive back in Jupiter until almost midnight, minutes before turning fifty.

Five hours later, he was up and at it, though being an early riser does have its drawbacks.

"I don't have many friends who like the morning as much as I do," Orr said, "so I have to wait a few hours until I can call anybody."

When he's home in Boston, more often than not, he's in his downtown office by 6 a.m.

An so it goes for Bobby Orr at fifty.

"I feel fine, I feel great and I probably wouldn't think too much about being fifty if everybody didn't keep reminding me of it," he said with a laugh.

Orr isn't a big birthday guy, or if he is he doesn't let on. He planned on having a few friends join him and his family (wife Peggy and sons Brent, 21, and Darren, 24) for dinner at their Florida home. Beyond that, it was no big deal, though it did give him pause for thought.

"I was at a Bruin game not long ago," Orr said, "and I saw

Johnny Bucyk there. I was thinking I've known the Chief for thirty-two years now. That's a lot of years, a lot of time."

Truth be told, Orr turning fifty probably make his fans feel older than it does him. To them, he'll always be the crewcut kid who revolutionized the game during nine glorious years with the Bruins (1966–67 through 1974–75) before being cut down in his prime at age twenty-seven.

But not before leading the Bruins to two Stanley Cups, winning two NHL scoring titles (a feat done neither before nor since by an NHL defenseman), establishing a host of scoring records, collecting three league MVP awards, earning eight defenseman awards and nine All-Star Team berths, and, of course, changing the role of defensemen in the game. There were great offensive blueliners before Orr, but none so dynamic, nor as consistently involved in the offensive zone.

The years since then have been kind to Orr. He hasn't aged gracefully so much as he has hardly aged at all. He's tanned, fit, and trim, with a wide smile and a firm handshake. He's always impeccably dressed, whether it's in his business uniform or his casual golfing attire. He works at taking care of himself. Orr is fastidious about his diet, avoiding junk food like the plague. He doesn't drink. He exercises regularly, going for walks when he can, walking on the treadmill when he can't.

Of course, given the injury-ravaged knees that cut short one of the most brilliant careers in NHL history, there are limitations.

"I'm not in real pain," Orr said. "The knees give me some discomfort. They ache sometimes and I am restricted in what I can do. I look awkward, I look funny when I walk sometimes. When I sit down, I have to get them out in front of me. I can't bend them. But considering all I went through, it's not too bad. Most of the time I'm really comfortable."

Literally and figuratively.

Orr is wealthy. Worldly and wise, too, which wasn't always the case when the naive young man from Parry Sound,

Ontario, blindly put trust in his first agent, Alan Eagleson, who went on to become a convicted felon. By the time Orr's glorious career was finished, so too was his bankroll.

But through the sometimes difficult transition of his non-playing days, Orr reconstructed a worthy financial empire and currently has lucrative deal with such companies as General Motors, Doubletree Guest Suites, MasterCard, and Reebok. He also spends a large amount of time doing charity work, much of it tied to golf tournaments.

And now, for the first time since he was a player, Orr is, surprisingly, back in the hockey mainstream. This summer will mark his second anniversary in the agent business.

"I'm enjoying it," Orr said. "It's a competitive business, but I enjoy competition. I also enjoy working with the kids, seeing that they get the help they need."

Orr doesn't negotiate contracts, but he has input with those who do. He's heavily involved in recruitment, going everywhere to solicit new clients and look after existing ones. For those who know him, they're not surprised at how passionate he is about his work. That's his nature — it's all or nothing. 'I can't be in this just to be on the letterhead," he said. "And I'm certainly not ready to retire."

His retired friends in Florida like to give him the gears. They say, "You don't have a j-o-b, do you? You're not really going to w-o-r-k, are you?"

"They won't even say the words," Orr laughed. "They just spell them."

But his closest friends were more than a little surprised when Orr and some business buddies in Boston purchased the Woolf agency. They wondered how he would react to the vagaries of the business — losing clients to other agencies, not getting clients after romancing them, and the hissing wars with NHL executives. Is this something a hockey icon does? Apparently, yes.

"There are a lot of good people in the industry," Orr said. "My attitude is . . . that we're going to do for our clients what we say we are going to do. And if a player leaves us because we haven't done our job properly, shame on us. If

Manager Art Ross with star players Cooney Weiland (left), Dit Clapper, and Eddie Shore.
— Hockey Hall of Fame

Mel "Sudden Death" Hill earned his nickname during the 1939 Stanley Cup semifinals when he scored three dramatic overtime goals to help the Bruins sink the New York Rangers.
— Hockey Hall of Fame

The Bruins' famous Kraut Line of Bobby Bauer, Milt Schmidt, and Woody Dumart. In 1939–40 they finished one-two-three in league scoring. Schmidt finished on top with 52 points; Bauer and Dumart each collected 43. — Hockey Hall of Fame

*Babe Siebert joined Eddie Shore to form
one of the best defensive duos in the NHL.*
— Hockey Hall of Fame

*Eddie Shore was the only defenseman
to capture the Hart Trophy four times.
He led Boston to Stanley Cup victories
in 1929 and 1939.* — Hockey Hall of Fame

*Aubrey "Dit" Clapper patroled right wing
and defense for the Bruins for two decades.
He served as player-coach during his final
two seasons as a Bruins player.*
— Hockey Hall of Fame

*Milt Schmidt was with the Bruins as
a player, coach, general manager, and
executive from midway through the
1936–37 season until 1973.*
— Alexandra Studio

Jerry Toppazzini scored 25 goals for the Bruins in 1957–58. — Hockey Hall of Fame

After starring with Detroit, Chicago, and Toronto, goaltender Harry Lumley joined the Bruins for three seasons late in his career. He was inducted into the Hockey Hall of Fame in 1980.
— Turofsky

Ralph "Cooney" Weiland centered the Bruins' famed Dynamite Line. He played on Cup–winning teams in his rookie season (1929) and in his final season (1939) with the Bruins.
— Hockey Hall of Fame

Frank Brimsek earned the nickname "Mr. Zero" after he made a sensational debut for the Bruins in 1938–39. Brimsek led the NHL in shutouts that season with 10 and captured the Calder Trophy.
— Hockey Hall of Fame

Four future Hall of Famers meet in a game in the 1950s. The Bruins' Leo Boivin (foreground) and Terry Sawchuk (#1) defend against Montreal's Rocket Richard (#9) and Jean Beliveau. — David Bier Studios

At the age of 16 years, 11 months, Bep Guidolin joined the Bruins for the 1942–43 season. He remains the youngest player ever to play in the NHL. — Guidolin Family

Purchased from Detroit in 1951, "Sugar" Jim Henry played for the Bruins until the end of the 1954–55 season.
— Hockey Hall of Fame

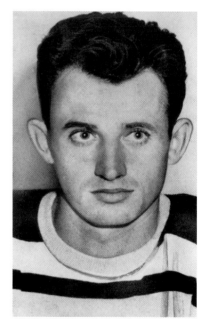

Pesky Leo Labine was a fan favorite in Boston throughout the 1950s.
— Hockey Hall of Fame

With 80 points in 1959–60, Bronco Horvath finished second in the scoring race to Chicago's Bobby Hull (81 points).
— Hockey Hall of Fame

BOBBY ORR

Bobby Orr won the Calder Trophy in 1967.
In this photo, he checks the Leafs' Bob Pulford.
— Hockey Hall of Fame

Orr and Montreal's Henri Richard
fight for the puck. — Hockey Hall of Fame

Orr played on two Stanley Cup–
winning teams, in 1970 and
1972, and captured the Conn
Smythe Trophy in both years.
— Hockey Hall of Fame

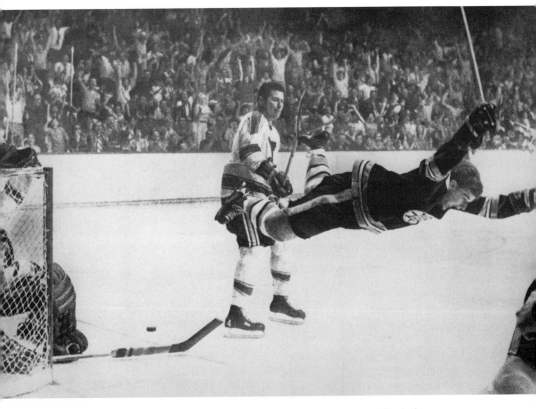

*Orr's famous
Cup-winning goal
against St. Louis
on May 10, 1970.*
— Ray Lussier, *Boston Herald*

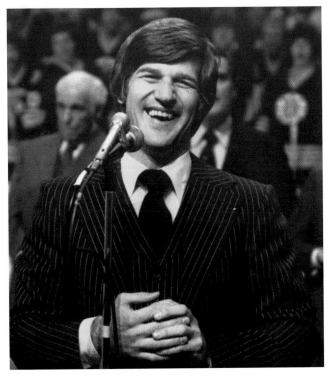

*No player ever
received a louder,
longer ovation than
Bobby Orr did on
his night at the
Boston Garden
in January 1979.*
— Hockey Hall of Fame

Orr is the only defenseman to capture the Art Ross Trophy as the league's top scorer — and he did it twice! — Robert B. Shaver

he leaves for any other reason, then we weren't going to have a good relationship with that player anyway."

Orr's experiences with Eagleson have colored not only how he goes about the agent business, but how he lives his life. Eagleson's guilty plea and jail sentence represented some closure to long-standing wounds. Orr will be watching intently when the Hall of Fame decides whether to expel Eagleson [it didn't have to, he resigned]. Orr was among a group of Hall of Famers, led by Gordie Howe, who vowed to withdraw if Eagleson wasn't expelled.

"I'm following the guy I think is the greatest player who ever played the game, a wonderful man," Orr said. "If Gordie had left, I would have left. Is that a difficult choice? Stay in the Hall with Eagleson or leave with Gordie Howe? That's an easy decision."

Meanwhile, Orr will work away on his new business. He said he enjoys going into players' living rooms and pitching his company's services. He wins some, loses some. There are things about the agent business that concern him — such as how young players are (as young as 14) when they're recruited — but that's not to suggest his company won't do it.

"I know we're not the first [agents] in the living room," he said. "But it's not just an agent thing, it's the system. Kids don't play Midget hockey anymore. They're playing Junior and that means they need advice, they have to make decisions."

If there's a better way for his industry to do it, Orr said, he's not opposed to exploring that. In the meantime, he has a job to do and he's doing it the same way he played — all out.

If Orr's fans feel cheated that his injuries prevented him from being all that he could be, Orr doesn't.

"Do I wish I could have played longer?" he said. "Absolutely. Do I dwell on what might have been? No. I played a reckless game and I enjoyed playing a reckless game. I paid the price to play the game recklessly.

"Honestly, I feel I'm a lucky guy."

Sinden, Cherry Gave Referee Grief

PERHAPS former NHL referee Bruce Hood chose the wrong profession, for he admits he never did like people yelling at him. Two of Hood's most severe and unrelenting critics were Harry Sinden and Don Cherry. Which of them was the most abusive? Hood says, "They were about equal, but over the long haul it was Sinden who gave me the most trouble."

It began when Sinden was player–coach of the Minneapolis club in the Central Hockey League. Night after night, game after game, Sinden chastised the young referee for one thing or another. He never let up.

One night, Carl Voss, the NHL's referee-in-chief, came to a game and Hood wanted to make a good impression. A well-handled game might be his ticket to the NHL. He asked the Minneapolis team captain to deliver a message to Sinden: Keep the chatter down, please, just for one game.

Sinden's reaction? He accosted Hood, saying, "Do your job right and you won't have to worry about me."

The abuse continued when both men were in the NHL. "Of all the players, coaches, and general managers I came across, Harry was the most vocal, the most abusive," Hood states. "It seemed that he and Cherry were having a contest to see who could foul-mouth me the most and the loudest."

Even two decades later, in his post-officiating career as a broadcaster, Hood felt Harry's wrath. During a playoff game in Buffalo in 1988, Sinden accused Hood of dumping on the Bruins during a telecast. "You were a horseshit official and now you're a horseshit commentator," he snarled.

Hood laughed and said, "Harry, you haven't got the guts to talk to your players. And you can't berate the officials because they're in their dressing room. So you take out your frustrations on me. Some class!"

Fists clenched, Sinden took a step toward Hood. Then he stopped and turned away.

In the same hallway on the following night, Sinden went berserk over the refereeing of Kerry Fraser. Boston coach Terry O'Reilly and assistant coach John Cuniff had to physically restrain Sinden. According to Hood, Sinden was like an animal, struggling and kicking. He aimed one foot at the door leading to the TV studio. He threw another at the guard outside the officials' dressing room.

"His attitude and actions were absurd," Hood wrote in his book *Calling the Shots*. "They shouldn't have been condoned. And the Boston media, many times, followed Sinden's example. Sometimes their opinions were so slanted in Boston's favor, it was ridiculous."

Harry Sinden takes Hood's comments in stride. He said recently, "I do regret my behavior in some situations during those years and would have acted less confrontational if I knew then what I know now.

"Having said that, nothing can change the fact that Bruce Hood was a poor to mediocre official during his time in the NHL. In those days coaches and general managers were less restrained in their remarks to referees and in many ways it acted as a 'check and balance' on their work. The way coaches and managers are acting today, however, is a much better way and less stressful on everybody including the officials. In my response to Hood's charges, if memory serves me right, he probably understates them. I believe I was even more demonstrative than he states."

Don Cherry isn't shy about how he feels about Bruce Hood.

"Let's see now, according to Bruce Hood, all of the Boston media is not any good. Don Cherry, coach of the year in the NHL, is not any good. Also not very good is the winner of the Stanley Cup, the Canada Cup, the Executive of the Year in the NHL [Harry Sinden], the winner of the Lester Patrick Award for his contributions to hockey in the U.S. [Harry again]. So we are all bad guys and Bruce Hood is a great guy? Hey, let's get real!"

The Famous Orr Photo

ABOUT that famous photo. You know the one — Bobby Orr flying through the air after scoring the Stanley Cup winner in overtime on May 10, 1970. Kudos to the photographer, a chap named Ray Lussier from the *Boston Herald*. Great timing, great photo.

But thumbs down on the ones who voted that moment as the greatest in NHL history.

It was the concluding moment of a series that matched the Bruins against an expansion team, the St. Louis Blues, a mediocre club that was only in the final series because the NHL dictated one of the six new franchises should be rewarded with a chance to win the Cup. All of the East Division teams except Toronto compiled more points and more goals than St. Louis did that year. Boston reached the finals with series victories over New York and Chicago while the Blues feasted on weak West Division foes.

One could name a dozen greater moments. Why then, did the folks at MasterCard select the Orr goal? Could it be that Bobby was a spokesman for the company?

The photo does lead to a neat bit of hockey trivia. Name the player who passed the puck to Orr for his winning goal. Then name the St. Louis player whose stick propelled Orr into the air. And name the St. Louis goalie who gave up the goal that ended the series.

Answers: Derek Sanderson, Noel Picard, and Glenn Hall.

Comments from a Candid Ref

BRUCE Hood, the former referee, has less than fond memories of three Bruins from the seventies.

He recalls Wayne Cashman as an intimidating player who liked to shove an opponent in the face and then sneer at him. When opponents went down, it looked like Cashman was ready to kick them. He attempted to intimidate the referees as well, by standing nearby, studying the blade of his stick, and muttering, "I'd like to gouge somebody's eyes out with this stick." Hood interpreted that to mean Cashman had the eyes of the referee in mind.

Hood readily admits that no NHLer ever handled the puck as brilliantly as Bobby Orr. At the same time he says that Orr could be most difficult on the ice. He'd verbally berate Hood, using the foulest language, for calls he made. And if he was sent to the penalty box, Orr would show his disdain by rushing into the box and throwing his stick down and slamming the door. Only after he got to know Bobby on a personal level at a summer hockey camp did Hood discover what a humble and classy individual he was.

As for Phil Esposito, Hood places him at the top of his list of players who liked to bitch and complain. Hood says, "Phil liked to bring the wrath of the Gallery Gods down on me and he knew just how to do it." Only after he was traded to the Rangers did Esposito mellow somewhat. "By then," says Hood, "after all those years of causing me grief, he was a pleasure to be around."

The Bruins' Bad Boy

WHEN Derek Sanderson graduated to the Boston Bruins from the Ontario Hockey League's Niagara Falls Flyers in 1967, he quickly established a reputation as the Bruins' number one "Bad Boy." That was quite an achievement considering Boston had "Terrible" Ted Green on the roster.

Sanderson became a clever playmaker and a Calder Trophy winner and he delighted in provoking opponents. He rated high on the list of hockey's all-time disturbers and he proved early on that he could stand up to all the heavyweights. In fact, Derek challenged the feared Orland Kurtenbach of the Rangers to a fight early in his rookie season. His attitude after the bout was, "you win some, you lose some, but you've always gotta show up."

Always sniffing around for trouble, Sanderson got himself involved in some unusual jackpots. He warned goalie Eddie Giacomin of the Rangers in one playoff game to "Watch out! I'm gonna put the next shot between your eyes." That crack set off one of the wildest brawls of the era. Giacomin went nose-to-nose with Sanderson before the next faceoff. "We're not playing hockey tonight, you turkey. We're being paid to get you." Sanderson grinned and said, "Take your best shot." When the puck was dropped, several Rangers did just that, attempting to pound him into the ice.

Sanderson, unlike most players, was not afraid of being punched out by the league's biggest enforcers. He said, "Hell, I like fighting. Maybe I'll get beat up but I'll get the guy eventually. What can happen to you in a fight? Lose a couple of teeth? I'll lose them eventually anyway."

Sanderson was capable of doing just about anything to agitate the opposition and often the fans as well. Do you recall the rubber chicken caper in St. Louis? A fan goaded Sanderson with a rubber chicken until he was forced to run for his life with a steaming Sanderson in hot pursuit. Turk chased the guy right into the stands and might have caught him if he'd stopped to take his skates off.

In a battle with Ray McKay of the Blackhawks, Sanderson ripped McKay's sweater off his back, scooped it up with the blade of his stick, held it triumphantly over his head, then tossed it disdainfully into the stands.

Why did the talented Sanderson choose to become hockey's bad boy, vilified in every rink but the Garden? "There are three things that make money in professional sports," he once said. "The first is talent, the second is points, and the third is color. With the Bruins, Orr and Esposito took care of the first two. That left me to look after the third."

Drinking and Drugs Almost Killed Sanderson

H E'S been clean for almost two decades now — free of drugs and booze, the addictions that almost killed him. It required eleven trips to drug and alcohol rehabilitation centers — and the words of a drunk he met in Central Park — before he won the battle.

Derek Sanderson, once a proud Bruin, once the highest-paid athlete in the world, shudders when he thinks of how close he came to losing his life.

"I lost everything else," he says. "Blew every cent. Lost my dignity, my self-respect, my friends. Lost my mind and my body. Terminated a great career."

"It was the age of drugs," he told reporter Earl MacRae, "and I got caught up in it. Cocaine made me feel like a genius. I became a drug addict as well as an alcoholic. I was a short step from death. In 1979, I was down and out in New York, sleeping in parks and flop houses. One night I tried to mug a drunk in Central Park. Tried to wrestle his bottle away from him. He fought me and told me to screw off. I said to him, 'Hey, do you know who I am?' He pulled away and answered, 'Yeah, you're a bum, a loser just like me.' Those words made me snap. He was right. I was a weak person with no strength of character, no guts to say no to the addictions that were destroying me. There were the blackouts, the nausea, the mood swings. That night I fell to my knees and prayed to God. I said, 'Please. Dear God, save me, please save me.'"

It was a turning point in Sanderson's life. With the help of people at the rehab centers, he kicked the habit and became a much different person. He promised himself — and God — that he would help others who were trapped in a world of drugs and alcohol.

Many of his friends didn't believe the promise would be kept. Sanderson, after all, was once called the Joe Namath of hockey. He was a charming playboy with unlimited funds. He lived the lifestyle of a rock star.

In 1972, he went from a third-line centerman with the Bruins, a $75,000 chattel, to the highest-paid player in pro sport when the WHA's Philadelphia Blazers made the grave mistake of offering him $2.6 million to jump leagues. But what did the owner of the Blazers know? He once asked his coach, "How come the players don't work from nine to five like my truck drivers do?"

Sanderson was never shy about spending the money. He treated a number of friends to a trip to Hawaii, then phoned his agent, Bob Woolf, to complain about the lack of hot water in his room. He'd buy clubs for a round of golf and then give the clubs to his caddy. He had glamorous girlfriends like actress Joey Heatherington. He bragged about getting caught in the rain one day. To avoid the drops, he walked into a car dealership and purchased a Rolls-Royce. Earl McRae says he'd carry $1,500 in $100 bills in his wallet and try to pay for a $4.50 cab ride with one of them.

No Swollen Head
for Brad Park

E VEN as a pee-wee player, Brad Park received a lot of attention. A team coached by his father, Bob Park, captured the grand championship of the famous Quebec International Pee-Wee Tournament. Park and Syl Apps, Jr., were the best players on the club.

Park went on to a sensational career with the Toronto Marlboros in junior hockey and was drafted second overall by the New York Rangers in the 1966 draft.

In his second NHL season he became an impact player for the Rangers. He was named to the All-Star Team — unusual for one so young — and he admits he was feeling pretty good about himself. Who wouldn't?

By then Park had bought a house in Toronto. One day in the off-season he was having his driveway measured by a contractor. He wanted an estimate on a paving job and he noticed that the young man taking the measurements kept glancing up at him. Finally he said, "Hey, aren't you Brad Park, the hockey player?"

Brad grinned and confessed that he was indeed Brad Park.

The young man said, "Thought so. You know, when you were a Marlboro I went to most of your games at Maple Leaf Gardens. My kids went, too. You were great, their favorite player."

"That's nice to hear," Park said, smiling.

"Say, Brad, you mind if I ask you something?"

"Not at all," said Park.

"What are you doing now?"

Park would laugh about the incident years later. "It's hard to get too puffed up about yourself with guys like that around. He didn't even know I'd made the NHL."

Park enjoyed a brilliant career, first with the Rangers and then with the Bruins. And in 1972, he was one of the key performers for Team Canada, coached by Harry Sinden, when they edged the Soviet Nationals in the famous eight-game series.

In 1982–83, Park and the Bruins were riding high. The club rolled to 50 wins and 110 points for the best record in hockey. In the Adams Division playoffs, the Bruins swept past Quebec and then Buffalo. Park scored the winning goal in overtime in Game Seven to propel his team to the Conference finals. But the Bruins were ousted from further playoff action by the Islanders' Mike Bossy, who scored four times in an 8–4 triumph in Game Six. The Islanders went on to capture the Stanley Cup, their fourth in a row.

After eight seasons as a Bruin, at age 35, Park declined to make a commitment to the club for the following season. He'd seen his friend Wayne Cashman fuming at his lack of ice time during the previous season, growing resentful and bitter. Park didn't want to see his own career end on a similar note. He decided to move on.

In a stunning mid-summer move, Park signed a two-year pact with the Detroit Red Wings as a free agent.

Harry Sinden screamed foul. He claimed Park had obligations to the Bruins for at least one more season and possibly two. He said the Bruins would take Park and the Red Wings to court if necessary.

Some say that Park was lured to Detroit not only by a handsome contract but by the gift of a couple of pizza franchises. "But please don't mention that on *Hockey Night in Canada*," Red Wing general manager Jimmy Devellano asked me at the time. "Otherwise, all of our star players will be demanding franchises."

Park finished out his playing career in Detroit, and retired in 1985. During the 1985–86 season he replaced Harry Neale as Red Wing coach, only to be replaced himself by Jacques Demers before the 1986–87 season.

Incidentally, Sinden never did receive compensation for Park's services, just as he was left empty-handed when Bobby Orr left for Chicago years before.

Bruins Among First to Suspect Eagleson

WHEN Don Awrey was out of work, after sixteen years of exceptional NHL service — ten with the Bruins — someone suggested he call the NHL Players Association for advice and assistance. Perhaps Alan Eagleson, the executive director, would be of some help.

"What a joke," Awrey told his friend Russ Conway, who covered hockey for the *Eagle-Tribune* in Lawrence, Massachusetts. "Eagleson won't talk to me. He only helps the players he represents — the ones who voted to keep him in as boss of the association — guys like Bobby Clarke and Tony Esposito."

Dallas Smith, another popular ex-Bruin, had echoed Awrey's comments back in the mid-seventies. This was after Bobby Orr, with Eagleson orchestrating the move, was allowed to leave Boston in 1976 for Chicago — with no compensation to the Bruins. ("We didn't get anything but a lot of grief following that move," Harry Sinden once recalled.)

Smith said ruefully, "Sure, it was okay for Bobby to jump to Chicago with no compensation. When I thought of moving to another club, Eagleson said I couldn't do it. Not without players coming the other way. Go figure."

Veteran goaltender Andy Moog also had a beef about the union boss: Eagleson's long-standing objection to salary disclosure. The players wanted salaries made public; the NHL, and Eagleson, didn't want it. "Eagleson said it was nobody's business what a player earned," said Moog. "I always thought if salaries were revealed there'd be much more competition among the clubs trying to sign players. It's common sense."

Gerry Cheevers recalled a contract Eagleson had negotiated for him. "The guy got me, like, $1,500 extra, and then he charged me something like $3,000 for his services. That meant I lost money on that deal."

139

Conway recalls that Terry O'Reilly, a former Bruins captain, told him in 1977 that the team owners had Eagleson in their back pocket. At a meeting of player reps, when O'Reilly challenged Eagleson on an important issue, Eagleson spat back, calling O'Reilly's questions "ridiculous and stupid."

"I quit as the Bruins' player rep that very day," snorted O'Reilly. "He was so sarcastic, so arrogant. From then on, whenever he came into the Bruins' dressing room, I walked out."

For almost two decades, the Bruins' Mike Milbury failed to understand how Eagleson was allowed to operate with so many obvious conflicts of interest.

No shrinking violet, and college-educated, Milbury boldly asked the tough questions: How could Eagleson run the NHLPA while acting as an agent for about 150 players? How could he run the Canada Cup tournaments while doing all the other things he did? Did the NHLPA adhere to sound accounting procedures? If so, could the players see the books? Why did Eagleson rebuff players who turned to him for help, unless they were his clients? How come hockey salaries were so low compared with those of other sports? Why did he endorse a merger with the upstart WHA when it surely killed competition for the players? Milbury's questions, for the most part, went unanswered or were answered in gobbledy-gook.

Gregg Sheppard, another former Bruin, loathed Eagleson and his modus operandi. He thought the situation was appalling. Sheppard wanted to know what happened to profits from the Canada Cup series. And why Eagleson was so friendly with most of the owners, as well as (then) NHL president John Ziegler.

Bruin defenseman Brad Park, a union vice president, complained that union meetings amounted to Eagleson's yes-men approving whatever Eagleson suggested.

Phil Esposito recalled Eagleson recruiting him to endorse the proposed merger with the WHA. Esposito was against the merger until Eagleson assured him NHL player pensions would be greatly increased if the two leagues merged because of huge expansion fees coming in from Edmonton, Winnipeg, Quebec, and Hartford. Later, when Esposito asked Eagleson how much of the $24 million in expansion fees went to the players' pension fund, he got a garbled answer. "I still don't know what we got out of it," Espo told Russ Conway.

Mike Gillis, a former Bruin and a client of Eagleson's, was bilked out of more than $40,000 of insurance money after he suffered a career-ending injury (a broken leg) in 1984. Conway claims that the insurance company involved had already agreed to settle the Gillis claim for $275,000 in 1986. But Eagleson led Gillis to believe he would have to hire outside lawyers to battle for the money. Gillis was told he'd have to agree to pay Eagleson 15 percent of the benefits. Of course he complied.

The mysterious business practices of Alan Eagleson, the NHLPA's executive director who often reminded one of a mad dictator, prompted Conway to embark on an investigation that went deep into Eagleson's shady past, revealing shocking evidence of skullduggery, deceit, and corruption. Eventually, Conway's series of articles on the subject, and his subsequent book, *Game Misconduct*, would help lead to Eagleson's downfall and earn Conway a runner-up spot for a Pulitzer Prize. Conway received much help from former NHL star Carl Brewer and his partner, Susan Foster.

Criminal charges against Eagleson were filed on both sides of the border after a seven-year investigation. The union boss was brought to trial in Ontario (almost three years after he was indicted in the U.S.) and convicted of fraud that had the effect of skimming thousands, perhaps hundreds of thousands of dollars from hockey players' pensions. He was sentenced to eighteen months in jail. The day before the Canadian sentencing, an American judge in Boston convicted Eagleson of mail fraud and fined him $1 million. By then he'd been barred from practicing law. He was soon shorn of his highest honor, the Order of Canada, and he resigned as an "honored member" of the Hockey Hall of Fame. He served a few months in a minimum security prison.

Conway called the Eagleson case "the biggest scandal to hit major pro sport since the White Sox threw the 1919 World Series."

And many of the Bruins were among the first to be aware of it.

Espo's Wild Ride

IT was a Ron Harris check that put Phil Esposito and the Boston Bruins out of the 1973 playoffs. Harris, a tough Ranger defenseman, sent Esposito to a Boston hospital, where doctors treated him for torn knee ligaments.

The next morning, when his teammates came to his room to visit, they told him they were planning a windup party at a nearby tavern.

"Gee, I wish I could make it," Espo sighed, "but the doctors tell me I'm going to be in here for a few more days."

"Oh, you're going to make it, all right," laughed Bobby Orr. "We're coming back to get you."

That evening, the Bruins paid Phil another visit. This time they had a plan. They distracted the nurses on duty with a wild story about a man outside who reportedly had been riddled with bullets. The nurses scurried around looking for the wounded man while the Bruins went to work. Orr and Dallas Smith wheeled Esposito's bed out of the room and pushed it down the corridor to the service elevator.

Down on the main floor, they ran into a problem. The metal railing on Espo's hospital bed made it too wide for the exit ramp. The players quickly dislodged the railing and tossed it aside. They were on their way to the party.

The Bruins hurried down the street, some pushing, some pulling on the bed and its famous patient.

As the reached an intersection, Orr shouted, "Signal a left, Phil, signal a left!" And Esposito's arm shot out from under the sheets to make the appropriate gesture.

Safely arriving at the party, Esposito became the center of attention. His mates poured him a little refreshment to fortify him for the return trip.

The party over, the Bruins wheeled Esposito back to the hospital where they found staff members milling about. One of them had discovered the broken railing and had compiled a bill for damage to hospital property, a bill of several hundred dollars.

"Who's going to look after this?" the man asked.

Orr and Smith examined the bill, then looked down at Esposito, who had nodded off to sleep. Gently, they slipped the bill into his pajama pocket.

Middleton Becomes a Gem

WHEN Rick Middleton joined the Boston Bruins in 1976 he was all flash and no substance. Like a lot of hotshot goal scorers he was terrible defensively. The Rangers realized his limitations and, at Phil Esposito's urging, were happy to trade him to the Bruins in return for Espo's old pal, Ken Hodge.

Fortunately, Middleton wound up in the lap of Don Cherry, a coach who was determined to make him play well in both ends of the rink. Cherry hammered, cajoled, threatened, and pleaded with Middleton, forcing him to become a complete player. And in time, he did.

People would eventually look back on the trade as one of the best the Bruins ever made. Hodge faded badly as a Ranger and was gone from the NHL less than two seasons after the trade. Middleton blossomed as a Bruin and scored 402 goals while wearing the B. Surely someday he'll be a Hall of Famer.

"Defensively, he could pick your pocket," Brad Park says. "Offensively, he could turn you inside out."

Barry Pederson, Middleton's linemate, said he used to commiserate with opposing defensemen when Middleton was in his heyday. "It had to be the scariest feeling in the world backing up and having Ricky come at you. He never made the same move twice. So many of them were left grabbing at air."

Middleton was quick to credit Cherry for his self-improvement.

"I promised Grapes a case of champagne if we won the Stanley Cup," he said. "Too bad it never happened."

Brad Park says Cherry was on Middleton's back all the time when he first joined the Bruins. "I remember the time Grapes gave us an optional practice. Cash (Wayne Cashman) and I skipped the workout and so, apparently, did Middleton. When we came to the Garden the following day, Cherry had Middleton up against a wall and was screaming at him. 'An optional practice is for guys like Park and Cashman,' he shouted. 'Not for some 23-year-old bleepety-bleep.'"

Cherry said proudly, "He turned out to be somethin', didn't he? Somethin' special, I mean. Ricky turned out to be one of the best players in the NHL. Maybe I didn't get the champagne, but after I left the Bruins I did receive a thank-you note from Middleton's parents. That was just as good."

Forbes Battles Boucha with Tragic Results

ON January 4, 1975, the Boston Bruins and Minnesota North Stars clashed at the Met Center in Minneapolis. While the Bruins were enjoying one of their best seasons ever, the North Stars were at the bottom of the NHL standings. The team was made up of average players with a few exceptions — Cesare Maniago, Dennis Hextall, and hometown favorite Henry Boucha.

During the first period Boucha tried to carry the puck out of the corner when Bruin sophomore Dave Forbes, fighting to stay with the team, checked him heavily against the boards. Boucha, smarting from an elbow in the face, turned and decked Forbes with one punch. Referee Ron Wicks handed both players minor and major penalties. In the box, the hot tempered opponents traded insults for the duration of their penalties. Someone heard Forbes threaten to shove his stick down Boucha's throat.

When the penalties expired, both players returned to the ice, glaring at each other and exchanging trash talk. Boucha had started toward his team's bench when Forbes skated alongside and lashed out at him while still holding his stick, catching Boucha totally by surprise. The butt end of Forbes' stick opened a deep cut over Boucha's right eye and the Minnesota player fell to the ice. Forbes fell on top of him and continued to throw punches perhaps unaware that his opponent was seriously injured. The linesmen and other players intervened and when peace was restored Boucha was hustled away on a stretcher. The cut over his eye required 30 stitches. Wicks ejected Forbes from the game for "deliberate attempt to injure."

The following day, a remorseful Forbes, who never received more than 30 minutes per season in penalties, apologized, and Boucha graciously accepted. NHL President Clarence Campbell suspended Forbes for ten games, considered a severe sentence at the time. But both players had bigger problems to face.

Within days, Boucha complained of impaired vision and further X-rays revealed a fracture at the base of his right eye socket. Despite remedial surgery, the eye still did not rotate fully within the socket. In time, he returned to hockey, but visual problems continued to haunt him. His goal production fell off dramatically, and he was soon gone from the game.

Forbes, meanwhile, was indicted by a grand jury in Minnesota for aggravated assault with a dangerous weapon (a hockey stick) and was brought to trial, the first action of its kind in professional sport. His trial ended in a hung jury and he was set free.

In January 1976, Henry Boucha filed a $3.5 million civil suit against Dave Forbes, the Boston Bruins, and the NHL for damages sustained during this incident. In the fall of 1980, a $1.5 million out-of-court settlement was reached, the largest settlement ever reached for an injury sustained during a sporting event of any kind.

Big Bad Bruins Meet
Big Bad North Stars

URING the 1970s, some NHL teams acquired nicknames that personified their style. There were the "Broad Street Bullies" in Philadelphia, "Les Glorieux" in Montreal, and the "Big Bad Bruins." The Bruins iced some very tough, physical players in the seventies, among them ornery Wayne Cashman, "Dirty" Derek Sanderson, "Terrible" Ted Green, and the combative "Tasmanian Devil," Terry O'Reilly. Some of coach Don Cherry's favorites were bruisers John Wensink, Stan Jonathon, and Bobby Schmautz. Even the legendary Bobby Orr displayed a bit of a mean streak occasionally, as did goaltender Gerry Cheevers, who used stick, hip, and glove to discourage those who invaded his crease.

During the Big, Bad Bruins era, visiting teams warming up for a game in the cosy confines of the Boston Garden had an eerie feeling that something bad was about to happen to them. And invariably it did. That's why opposing players would sometimes complain of headaches, nausea, and fatigue on the eve of a game with the Bruins. "It's just the Boston Garden flu," their teammates would tell them. "Get over it."

Even the toughest old birds were apprehensive about games at the Garden. Dave "The Hammer" Schultz complained he didn't sleep very well in the days leading up to a game with the Bruins. "Our tough guys [in Philadelphia] are just as tough as the Bruins' tough guys," Schultz would say. "The difference is, four of their tough guys are completely nuts."

In the late seventies, big John Wensink engaged in a lively scrap with one of the young North Star players in a game at Minnesota. While being ushered from the ice with a game misconduct, Wensink heard someone on the Minnesota bench tell him to go f—— himself. Wensink was surprised because the North Stars were known as a passive team, a club easily intimidated. He raced over and stood directly in front of the Minnesota bench, waving his arms and verbally challenging anyone to jump on the ice. The North Stars may have hurled insults at Wensink, but none of them dared to leap over the boards to meet his challenge. After the game, Don Cherry described Minnesota as "a chicken team."

By the early eighties, the North Stars were able to ice a young, talented team, but they still suffered from a reputation as pacifists. The North Stars had never won a game at the Boston Garden. Their new coach, Glen Sonmor, was a firebrand who knew that his team would have to establish a reputation for "showing up" around the league. And what better opponent to begin with than the Big Bad Bruins. That night he told his players they'd better not back down from anything or anyone. He reminded them how John Wensink had once caused them much embarrassment.

One of the enforcers on Sonmor's club was Jack Carlson, a noted ruffian who had played one of the Hanson brothers in the Paul Newman movie *Slapshot*. When asked what would have happened on the night Wensink challenged the entire Minnesota bench if he'd been a North Star, Carlson said, "Well, if I was there and Sonmor was the coach I would have had to act fast just to beat my coach onto the ice."

In his pre-game sermon to his North Star players, Sonmor indicated that by employing their new strategy, they "might not win the game but there will be favorable residual effects for the North Stars." What a prophet he turned out to be.

On February 26, 1981, a Boston–Minnesota game was only seven seconds old when two fights broke out, one between Boston's Keith Crowder and Minny's Steve Payne, the other featuring mild-mannered Bobby Smith and the Bruins' Steve Kasper. Smith was a very talented player, not known for his physical play, but on that night, new reputations were about to be established. These fights were just the beginning.

There were numerous other battles during the game, including a brawl that took place in the aisle between the penalty box and the Bruins' bench. That one started when the Bruins' Keith Crowder, sitting in the box, punched Minnesota's Greg Smith, who was en route to the locker room after being penalized. The benches cleared and a scrum developed in the aisle. In all, 210 minutes of penalties were called, and 12 players were ejected with game misconducts. Less than half a period of hockey had been played.

When the game finally ended, a new record was established for most penalty minutes in a regular season game — 406. Referee Dave Newell issued 30 minor penalties, 32 major penalties, 8 10-minute misconducts, and 13 game misconducts. Boston won the game 5–1, extending Minnesota's winless streak on Boston ice to 35 games. Minnesota's record at the Garden fell to 0–28–7.

But the war didn't end there. After the game, Harry Sinden told reporters, "Minnesota had more penalties tonight than in their 13-year history in this building. Among hockey people, Minnesota has gained a reputation as the most chicken team ever developed. From what we know of Minnesota teams, they are a no-guts team."

Glen Sonmor fired back, "[Bruin coach Gerry] Cheevers was yapping at our players, and asking about the heart of Bobby Smith. If he wants to check the heart of anybody in our organization, let him start with mine. We've got a corridor right down by our dressing room in Minnesota. Tell Cheevers to meet me down there and I'll gladly accommodate him. And tell him to bring a basket to carry his head home in. I've had it up to here with him."

Sonmor insisted that the North Stars franchise turned the corner the night they stood up to the Big Bad Bruins.

Two days after the game, Minnesota general manager Lou Nanne called for the abolishment of fighting in the NHL. "Any time the league's highly skilled players get involved in fighting, the fans are the ones who get cheated," he said.

By chance, Minnesota and Boston met in the first round of the Stanley Cup playoffs that season. Boston had home ice advantage in the five-game series, but to everyone's surprise, Minnesota won the first two games at the Boston Garden, 5–4 in overtime in Game One, followed by a 9–6 win in Game Two. (The 15 combined goals scored in game two tied an NHL playoff record set in 1973 when Chicago edged Montreal 8–7.) In Game Three, Bobby Lalonde scored back-to-back goals for the Bruins in the third period, but it was too little, too late. The North Stars had scored four first-period goals and coasted to a 6–3 decision, eliminating Boston in three straight.

Do You Know Whom I Am?

AT the height of his success in the seventies, he was drinking champagne from the Stanley Cup. He owned forty-five Edwardian suits, parts of three popular bars, dated beautiful women, and his biggest worry was finding someone reliable to drive him around in his Rolls-Royce.

Everybody knew Derek "Turk" Sanderson, the playboy center for the Boston Bruins, the Joe Namath of hockey, possibly the game's most publicized player. In the early seventies, daring Derek played a speaking role in an X-rated film showing in Montreal. There was a "Date with Derek" contest that drew thousands of entries. The winner, Mabel Hocking, a 72-year-old grandmother, gazed adoringly at Derek across a table at his Bachelors III nightclub.

He was a first rate player, a skilled penalty killer, and a former Calder Trophy winner. But with the Bruins, he played in two huge shadows, those of Phil Esposito and Bobby Orr. Still, he loved being a Bruin and the fact he was idolized by the fans, grandmothers included.

Until the World Hockey Association came along, that is.

In 1972, Boston teammate John "Pie" McKenzie urged him to jump to the Philadelphia Blazers of the WHA.

"Nah, I don't want to go," said Sanderson. "I love Boston and everybody here loves me."

"What are the Bruins paying you? I hear seventy-five grand."

"Yeah, but we're talking. I'm asking for eighty grand."

"The Blazers will pay a hell of a lot more than that. At least talk to these people."

"I guess that wouldn't hurt. Tell them to come see me."

Sanderson describes the subsequent meeting with the owners of the Blazers as the most amazing negotiating session of his life.

"Right off the bat they offered me a couple of million to sign. That got my attention. I was so stunned I had them write the figures down. It looked like a long distance phone number. When I hesitated for a few seconds to collect my thoughts they raised the offer to $2.6 million. I asked them to write that figure down, too.

"I said, 'Wait a minute. I don't know you guys. If I sign this you'll probably sell the team down the road.'

"They said, 'Derek, we won't sell the team and if we do, we'll make sure you sanction the sale.'

"Geez, that was something. So then I said, 'You'll probably trade all my friends.'

"And they said, 'Derek, we'll make sure you approve all trades.' I'd never heard of such a thing.

"Then I said, 'I'm not much on flying. All those road trips across the country . . .'

"And they said, 'Hey, just play home games.'

"Before we finished I even had them add a clause to the contract, 'The coach must not speak harshly to the players.' You see, I knew about the coach, Phil Watson, and his reputation for screaming at the guys.

"What did I do next? I took the contract to the Bruins and showed it to Mr. Adams, who had always been good to me. He shook his head in disbelief. Then he said, 'Derek, I'm sure we can find a way to pay you the eighty thousand you asked for.'

"I said, 'Well, that's very nice and I'd like to stay in Boston. But I know Mr. Mulcahy who handles contracts doesn't think much of me. If I'm going to sign I'd rather sign with your son, Weston, Jr., if that's all right.'

"So I walk down the hall into Westy, Jr.'s office and I've got two contracts with me, one for eighty grand and one for $2.6 million. While I'm pondering my next move, Mr. Mulcahy sticks his head in the door, sees me standing there, and says, 'Sanderson, I still don't think you're worth eighty grand a season.'

"That did it. I grabbed the Philadelphia contract, walked out, and signed it.

"According to my agent, Bob Wolff, that signature made me the wealthiest athlete in the world."

Cashman a Ruffian and a Rogue

DESPITE the antics of Derek Sanderson, Mike Walton, and others, Wayne Cashman was the zaniest, if not the meanest and toughest, member of the Big Bad Bruins of the seventies.

"I knew I'd never be a 50-goal scorer so I spent my career doing what had to be done," Cashman told *Sports Illustrated* while toiling in the twilight of his career.

He played left wing on one of Boston's most prolific lines, with Phil Esposito at center and Ken Hodge on right wing. He was counted on to do the dirty work in the corners, and to get the puck by fair means or foul to Espo in the slot. Goaltender Gerry Cheevers says, "Cash was the greatest of all the guys from our era when it came to digging in the corners and along the boards. And if someone gave Orr or Espo a cheap shot Cashman would be there in an instant, throwing punches, exacting revenge."

When Cashman retired in 1983, he had served 1,041 penalty minutes to rank third among Boston sinners (behind Terry O'Reilly and Keith Crowder). At 38, he had served the Bruins well in 1,027 games, second only to Johnny Bucyk's club record of 1,436. When veterans Serge Savard of the Winnipeg Jets and Carol Vadnais of the New Jersey Devils bowed out of NHL hockey a few days before Cashman's final game, it made the Bruin left winger the oldest survivor of the Original Six teams.

Off the ice, he was a master of mischief. Once he broke his foot while swinging on a chandelier, and in 1970, after the Bruins won the Stanley Cup, he played traffic cop during the celebrations that followed. He stood in a Boston intersection waving cars in all directions until there was a mammoth snarl. Reluctantly, the cops arrested him and brought him to the station where he was told he could make one phone call. Did he phone his lawyer? No. A Chinese deliveryman showed up soon after his call with a steaming package in his arms. "Sweet and sour spare ribs and some egg rolls for Mr. Cashman," the man announced.

Cashman, like millions of others, was stunned on November 7, 1975, to learn the Bruins had traded his best pal Phil Esposito, along with Carol Vadnais, to the hated New York Rangers in return for Brad Park, Jean Ratelle, and Joe Zanussi. He organized a going-away party for his former mates in a Vancouver hotel room, and, before it was over, they had caused $2,000 in damages.

The following season, he assumed the Bruins' captaincy and the hijinks became less frequent. Johnny Bucyk, who'd been wearing the "C," returned from an injury, saw the leadership that Cashman was providing, and told him to keep it. General manager Harry Sinden would later say, "I don't think I could have dreamed of Cashman becoming such a leader."

He was durable enough to play in more than 1,000 games, third highest in team history. With 793 points, he ranks sixth on the list of Boston's all-time scorers behind Bourque, Bucyk, Esposito, Middleton, and Orr. And he holds the same position among playoff scorers.

A great player? Yes. A different kind of guy? You bet.

Even as a child he was unpredictable. One day on the family farm near Kingston, Ontario, where he grew up, he acquired a new pair of skates. Told by his parents not to wear them outside until the weather warmed up, young Cash waited one day until his parents went off somewhere. He opened all the windows, hooked up a hose, and flooded the kitchen floor with an inch of water. "When it freezes," he reasoned, "I'll skate inside."

Guidolin Does Not Leave Quietly

MOST hockey fans believe that Bep Guidolin, coach of the Bruins for twenty games in 1973 and for all of 1973–74 (the year they lost to Philadelphia in the Stanley Cup Finals), was fired by the Bruins.

Not so. Guidolin quit the club, one of the best in hockey, and later resurfaced as coach of the pathetic Kansas City Scouts.

Guidolin stormed out on the Bruins on May 27, 1974, hurling accusations that the team he coached was soft and lazy. He accused Harry Sinden of allowing Phil Esposito to "run the damn team." He had a number of caustic comments about some of his other charges. When Guidolin ordered winger Ken Hodge to "move your butt or you may not be around here much longer," Hodge is said to have replied, "Oh, I'm going to be around for some time but I'm not sure about you."

After Guidolin was hired by the Scouts for the 1974–75 season, at $45,000 ($15,000 more than his Boston contract), Harry Sinden told writer Earl McRae, "the problem with Guidolin is that he is very limited as a coach. He was good on conditioning and skating drills but he wasn't good at getting along with the players. He couldn't hack Esposito, he couldn't hack Sanderson or Walton. He said, 'Let's get rid of them.' Hell, they were all good hockey players. I'm not saying coaches should always love their players. I was a coach myself and they don't, but, hell, they have to try and understand them. Not Bep. He wouldn't bend."

Guidolin proved his toughness when he first took over the Bruins, extending practice times to ninety minutes, canceling days off and imposing bed checks and strict curfews. Hard-nosed old-time coaches like Toe Blake and Punch Imlach would have loved him. They might also have cautioned him that "what worked for us in the fifties and sixties doesn't mean squat in the

NHL today, when players earn fortunes and have plenty of teams seeking their services."

Guidolin's coaching idol was NFL legend Vince Lombardi. "Lombardi was one tough bastard," Guidolin once said. "He was like me, hot-tempered, tough."

Sinden sneered. "Bep was no Lombardi. Lombardi was intelligent. He could talk to his players. He wasn't shouting and screaming, he was communicating. Bep had none of that."

Don Cherry Reminisces

On His Junior Hockey Days in Barrie, Ontario

I remember the old Barrie Arena. It was one of those Ontario small-town arenas with those wooden seats. And cold! And it just felt like hockey, it smelled like hockey, if there is such a thing.

We won the Memorial Cup up there in 1953, it was unbelievable! First, we beat out St. Mike's — and our coach, Hap Emms, was the smartest man I ever played for. Well, him and Punch Imlach. Anyways, we were beating St. Mike's in the final game for the Ontario championship in Barrie — and I shouldn't say this 'cause it shows how mean Hap could be — but I saw Hap with this thing that looked like a book, all wrapped up like a lovely Christmas present.

So when the score got to be 5–1 or something like that, and there was about a minute to go in the game, he called Billy Dineen, who was a great guy and the captain of St. Mike's, to come over. And he says "Billy, give this little present to your coach." We all think that Hap is turning into a pretty nice guy. So Dineen took the present over and the coach opened it and the book cover read "How to Coach Hockey". Hap is smiling, the coach over there is livid, and Billy Dineen went nuts! He tried to jump over the boards and strangle every one of us. It was great!

Now, Hap was always doing stuff like that. We played in

Maple Leaf Gardens one day and he wouldn't tell us who the starting goalie was gonna be. So for the first five minutes of the warmup, Hap had someone hang a sweater in the net. We were skating around shooting at a sweater! Unbelievable! Oh, he was colorful. He could be mean but on the other hand he wouldn't let us play on Sunday afternoon because of his religious beliefs.

We had a great team in Barrie. When we came on the ice they played the *Dragnet* theme, because we were supposed to be mean guys. It would go DUN DUN DUN DUN and we'd be pumped. It was great. Hap made it great. He made hockey, and he sold the game. I say he was the best Junior coach of all time.

We won the Memorial Cup, but to tell the truth, I got a bigger kick out of winning the OHA title, the series leading up to the Cup. And I'll tell you why. After we won it, we were going back to Barrie along [Highway] 400, and all the farmers along the side of the road had lit big bonfires and were cheering us all the way home. They were moments that'll live forever, I'll tell you that.

I just thought of a great story. Do you remember Eric Nesterenko, a big winger who played for the Marlies? In my first year in Barrie, he came down the wing and shoved the puck through my legs. He sailed around me and rang one off the post. *The Globe* had a picture of it the next day. The paper said, "Don Cherry played 'Button, button, who's got the puck?'" Guess what Emms did to me? He actually drilled a hole in a puck, put some rope through the hole, put the rope around my neck and made me go to school that way. For a week I wore that puck around my neck. And for the rest of the winter I kept a puck in my coat pocket to remind me never to look at the puck but to play the man. By the end of the season, players would come down on me and show me the puck and make their move. But they might as well have picked it up and handed it to me, because I would always take the man. Always.

On Heeding Authoritarian Figures

No, I was never very good at that. Like in school I didn't listen to my teachers — not enough, anyway. And I got the strap a lot. I would not bow down to them. I remember one time, the principal said, "What did you do to so and so?" And I said, "I didn't do nothin'." And he said, "If you didn't do nothing then you must have done something. Say it right next time." But he didn't intimidate me. I said to him, "I still didn't do nothin'." And out would come the strap. The man loved his strap. I remember I had to open the door with my wrists because my hands hurt so much. So, yeah, I was a rebel, a cocky guy in school. But I never let my father know I got the strap. Now I know a lot of you people reading this are saying, "Yeah, yeah, because your father would give you twice as bad when you got home." No way! I didn't let him know because if he ever found out that anybody ever touched me with a strap, Mr. Jackson, our principal, would be dead meat. So I told my Ma when I got strapped, but made her promise not to tell Dad. And she would say, "I suppose if your principal plans to live to a ripe old age, maybe we'd better not tell him."

On the Skill Level of Today's Juniors

Well, I'm gonna be honest. I think today's Juniors can skate better than we did. They all seem to be bigger, and they can shoot harder. When I played you would have about three guys on a team who could wire a puck. Now if you have twenty guys, about nineteen can wire the puck. I don't think they handle the puck as well, though, and I don't think they are as smart as we were. That's just my personal opinion. I wonder what Bobby Orr must think when he goes to a kids' game and hears the coaches yelling like they do to the defensemen, "Pass it! Pass it! Move it! Move it!" I say you gotta let 'em handle the puck, that is why the Europeans handle the puck just a little better than us sometimes, because they handle it so much. You gotta let the guys handle the puck. Sure, they're bigger and they skate faster. But I'll say it again — not quite as smart.

Memories of Bobby Orr

How long is this book? I got so many Bobby Orr stories. First you have to remember that I played 16 years in the minors and I was playing when I was 36 years old. And this will really surprise you because at first I couldn't stand Bobby Orr. He stood for everything I was against. I was a big defenseman, and I would see him on TV sometimes, and I would think that this guy isn't a defenseman, this guy is a rover. He's all over the place.

I was playing for the Rochester Americans and we were playing in Boston one night. Well, we had a practice the next morning, right after the Bruins' practice. So I walk in early, and you have to remember that I've seen Gordie, I've seen the Rocket, I've seen 'em all. I'm like an old horse trainer — can't fool me. So I walk in and I saw Orr practicing and my mouth fell open. I could not believe it. It must have been like Sunny Jim Fitzsimmons when he saw Secretariat for the first time. I was mesmerized by the things he was doing. I had never seen anything like it and he was just jerkin' around. Nobody ever skated like him or handled the puck like him and he was just jerkin' around. Little did I know that four or five years later I'd be coaching him.

And you know what happened when I was coaching the Bruins — if we fell behind, we always knew Orr would be back to pop a couple in, and if we were ahead, he'd be there to slow the game right down. When he was killing a penalty, he could kill the whole penalty himself. He was incredible! You know how they would chase him out front, and he would go in behind the net, and when they chased him in behind the net, he went in front! He made monkeys of people.

The best goal I ever saw him score was when we were playing the Atlanta Flames and Bobby had the puck behind our net. No one would go in after him because they knew he'd make them chase him out front and they would never catch him. So they left him alone because they were tired of chasing him all game. So Bobby came out from behind the net real slow and started up the wing. He got to just inside their blueline and he began to pick it up — you know, he had four different speeds. Then, for some dumb reason, they all ran at him and he sifted by them all. Now he goes behind their net and their goaltender makes a stab at him and the goalie falls down! Bobby slips out in front and backhands the puck into the net while they are all laying on the ice. And the type of guy he is, he's not a hot dog, he puts his head down as if to say, "Sorry, guys." And if you look at every goal he scored, it was almost as if he would be saying under his breath, "Sorry, guys, I really didn't mean to embarrass you like that."

Now, this is another true story, I know it is hard to believe, but it is true. The Bruins had flown out to L.A. and we're going on the ice to get a little sweat, shoot a few pucks, just to get the jet lag worked out. Carol Vadnais was first guy out, and it was dark because they didn't have all of the lights on. So he is the first out and I am the second, so we were just skating around waiting for the guys. Then Bobby comes out. Now, there were a bunch of pucks in the corner, just behind the goal line, and Bobby takes a puck, flicks it in the air, doesn't even look at the net at the far end, just flicks it and it lands in the top corner. Now, I don't know if I saw what I thought I saw so I go up to Vadnais and I say "Did you see what he did?" And Carol goes, "Geez, Grapes, I'm glad you said something. I don't believe it, either." Orr was supernatural.

Serge Savard said it best when he said, "There are players, there are stars, there are superstars, and then there is Bobby Orr." Bobby Clarke said he thought they should have had another league for him to play in, and Terry O'Reilly once said they should pass him around from team to team each year, to keep things fair.

How He Almost Worked for Ballard

After Harry fired me in Boston, I was still coach of the year. I was the king. So the job in Colorado appealed to me at the time. Maybe it was the $145,000 offer that appealed to me, because Harry had been paying me $40,000 in Boston. Not bad, eh? The Colorado offer was the highest paying offer, so I was gonna go there. I remember Billy Watters, who worked with Eagleson then, drew up the contract and I shook hands with Ray Miron, the general manager there. I remember shaking hands 'cause that's important when you're wheeling and dealing. So now I get a call — I was laying in bed that day and I can remember this as plain as day. The call was from Al Eagleson and he says, "Don, I just got a three-year contract for you from Toronto. It's for $150,000, a year, guaranteed, even if you get fired." My heart leaped because that was a great team in Toronto. Remember that team of '79–80, with Darryl Sittler, Lanny McDonald, Ian Turnbull, Mike Palmateer, and the Swedish guy, Borje Salming? It was a hell of a team, and Toronto wasn't too far from Kingston and my Ma.

But I said to Al, "No, I can't do it." And he screams, "What do you mean you can't do it?" I say, "Well, I just shook hands with Ray Miron so it's a deal." Eagleson is fumin'. He says, "I don't give a shit if you shook hands, I didn't shake on it. Don, this is unbelievable. People would die for a chance to coach the Leafs. Harold's been calling me every day." I said, "Al, I said I can't do it. I shook hands with the guy. I can't go back on my word." So anyways, I go to Colorado and ended up getting fired very quickly by Ray Miron. At the end of it, I said to Ma, "Ma, I am fired now, I could have been with Toronto, they were a great team. Ma, are you sure this shaking hands thing is good, you know, keeping to your word? I am beginning to wonder about it." And my mom smiled and said, "Don, it will all work out in the end, it will all work out in the end." And I was thinkin', "I don't know about that. Here I am unemployed for the second year in a row."

On His Television Career

After I got canned by Colorado, I get a call from a guy and he says, "Don, I'd like you to come to Toronto and do something for the CBC, for *Hockey Night in Canada*." I really didn't feel like it but the guy persuaded me to give it a shot. So I came down, and we did something, and I asked, "What are we gonna call it?" Someone said, "Let's call it 'Coach's Corner,'" so I say, "Okay, sounds good to me." So I read from a script and it was terrible. I did, I think, eight of those shows and they were all terrible. So I went back down to Denver, and they called from the CBC to say they really liked them, come back and do eight more. I thought they were kidding, but the next time we did them without the script and they were better. Then I got a chance to do color. I loved doing color. I would rather do color than Coach's Corner, but when I did, I would always get in too much trouble. One night Danny Gallivan and I were working together and the next day

Danny got a memo from one of our executive producers. It said we were being too frivolous and that they really wanted to have in-depth analysis. Now this was a game between Colorado and Toronto, who were both down in the tank back then. I remember at the end of the first period Danny said to me, "Well, Don, how did you like that period?" I laughed and said, "Well, Danny, the only star in this game so far has been the Zamboni driver." And Danny laughed and said, "Mr. Cherry, I would have to say that period was as shabby as a hobo's coat." So we both got letters saying that we had better stop trying to be funny. So then what happened was, they stopped me doing color, and I started doing Coach's Corner, and people seemed to like it. And you know, it proves that my mother was right all along. If I had coached the Leafs, I would have never gotten Coach's Corner. So always listen to your mother!

His Thoughts on Ron MacLean, His TV Sidekick

A lot of people ask me how I get along with him, and I say we think exactly opposite. He is a referee, which I can't stand, and he is from the West, which is another thing. And he doesn't mind Europeans, and everything. So we are exactly different. Then people ask if the show is scripted. Are you kiddin'? We never rehearse or script anything. In fact, in the openings, I have someone stand in for me, 'cause I don't wanna even rehearse the openings. If I do, I will screw it up. And if they ask me to do something over again, it is tough for me, because I am not a professional. I just do it. Anyway, MacLean is still there every week and I say he has come a long way from being a weatherman in Red Deer. Of course with me beside him, how could he not succeed?

On His Future

You know, that is a good question. I got told five years ago that I should get off TV, that my popularity is gonna start waning. Yeah, that's the word they used — waning. I remember I had to ask what that meant. But I am just gonna keep pluggin' along and doin' it. I am sure I'll be fired someday, there's no doubt about that. I have come pretty close about half a dozen times in the past. So I think I will be fired in two or three years, if not sooner. Every good thing must come to an end. I figure it's all gravy anyway. I never thought I would last this long. Geez, I remember the first month I was on, some of the CBC brass wanted to fire me. And that was umpteen years ago.

7

Bourque and O'Reilly Rule the Eighties

Grahame Deal
Nets Bourque

F OLLOWING a successful four-year career at the University of Denver, goaltender Ron Grahame, a Victoria, B.C. native, turned pro with the Macon Whoopees of the Southern Hockey League in 1973.

In 1974, he signed with the Houston Aeros of the World Hockey Association, arriving in Texas at the same time as the Howe family — Gordie, Colleen, Mark, and Marty.

Named to the All-Star team in his initial WHA season and as winner of the league's top goaltender award, Grahame caught the eye of the Boston scouts. Prior to the start of the 1977–78 season, Harry Sinden signed him as a free agent. Grahame performed well for the Bruins, compiling a 26–6–7 record.

But Sinden had a chance to snare the L.A. Kings' number one draft choice in 1979, if he'd give up Grahame. Sinden agreed to the deal.

The 1979 draft began with Colorado selecting defenseman Rob Ramage. Perry Turnbull, drafted number two, went to St. Louis, and Mike Foligno was taken by Detroit third overall. Washington, with fourth pick, grabbed Mike Gartner. Next, in order, Vancouver selected Rick Vaive, Minnesota opted for Craig Hartsburg, and Chicago, with seventh choice, snapped up Keith Brown.

Then it was Sinden's turn. With the King's first choice, number eight overall, he could have selected one of a dozen future stars, for the 1979 draft was rich in talent. Michel Goulet, Brian Propp, Mats Naslund, Dale Hunter, Kevin Lowe, and Mark Messier were still available. But Sinden plucked defenseman Ray Bourque off the roster of the Verdun junior team, giving the Bruins a player who would star for the next 20 years, a rearguard who would often be mentioned in the same breath as Bobby Orr. But it wouldn't have happened if Sinden hadn't traded a surplus netminder.

While Bourque was the big prize, Sinden scored repeatedly in the same draft, selecting defenseman Brad McCrimmon (15th), Keith Crowder (57th), Larry Melnyk (78th), goalie Marco Baron (99th), and Mike Krushelnyski (120th overall).

Bourque's Stats Are Truly Awesome

WHEN the Boston Bruins selected Raymond Jean Bourque eighth overall in the 1979 Entry Draft they had no idea he would score more goals and points in the next two decades than superstar offensive defensemen like Bobby Orr, Brad Park, and Larry Robinson.

But they knew they had a phenom when he set a record for points by a rookie defenseman and became the first non-goaltender in NHL history to win the Calder Trophy and a First-Team All-Star berth in his initial season.

In 1983–84 he became only the sixth defenseman in league history to score 30 goals in a season and the following year he won his first team scoring title.

In 1985–86 he played his 500th game and scored his 500th point. A year later, he won his second team scoring title and led all NHL defensemen in scoring, finishing tenth overall.

He captured his third team scoring title in 1987–88 and set a club mark for defensemen with a 19-game point-scoring streak. He led the league's defensemen in playoff scoring with 21 points.

In 1988–89, despite missing 20 games with a knee injury, he became the seventh defenseman in league history to score 200 goals. Early in the season he scored his 700th point, several weeks before playing in his 700th game.

The following year he scored his 800th NHL point, enjoyed a career high 6-point night against Vancouver in February, and led all NHL defensemen in playoff scoring.

In 1990–91 he won his fourth team scoring title and finished second among NHL defensemen in scoring. During the season he became only the fifth defenseman in history to reach the 900-point milestone.

In 1991–92 he became the third defenseman in league history to reach 1,000 points and the fourth to surpass 700 assists. He moved ahead of Bobby Orr as Boston's all-time leading goal scorer among defenseman. He led the Bruins in assists, points, and plus/minus.

The following year he passed Johnny Bucyk as the Bruins' all-time career assist leader with his 795th helper and became the second defenseman in league history to reach 800 assists.

In 1993–94 he led all NHL defensemen in scoring despite missing 12 games and was on the ice for 79 of 80 Boston's power-play goals. He recorded his 1,100th NHL point in October and played in his 1,100th NHL game in March. Midway through the season he became only the third NHL defenseman to score 300 career goals.

In 1994–95 he led the league in shots and became the second defenseman and seventh player in history to record 900 NHL assists. During the season he collected his 1,200th point.

In 1995–96 he hit the 20-goal mark for the ninth time in his career, was named MVP of the All-Star Game, and notched his 1300th career point in late March.

In 1996–97, he became Boston's all-time leading scorer with his 1,340th point and became only the fifth player in league history to reach 1,000 career assists (Gretzky, Howe, Dionne, and Coffey were the others).

At this point in his career, his points-per-game average (1.06) was marginally better than Gordie Howe and Stan Mikita's (both 1.05).

In 1997–98, he played in his 1,300th NHL game in October and recorded his 1,400th point in March. He scored 10+ goals for the 19th consecutive season. After 20 seasons as a Bruin, Bouque's stats include 1,372 games, 375 goals, 1,036 assists, and 1,411 points. He's in a fascinating duel, one that's been overlooked by the media, with Paul Coffey for the title of "hockey's highest scoring defenseman." As both men near the end of their careers, they opened the 1999–2001 season tied in career goals with 385. Coffey had a slight lead in assists, 1,102 to 1,083, and in points, 1,487 to 1,468. But Coffey's production has plummeted in the past couple of seasons while Bourque's has only slightly declined. In 1998–99 Bourque scored 8 more goals and 34 more points than Coffey. The betting is on Bourque to become the highest-scoring rearguard ever.

Bourque's amazing stats guarantee him a spot in the Hockey Hall of Fame soon after retirement. He has been rewarded for his exploits with lots of hardware: he has won the Calder Trophy, the Norris Trophy (five times), and the King Clancy Trophy. He has been named to the First All-Star Team 12 times (tied with Gordie Howe for most appearances) and to the second team five times. He helped fill a huge vacuum when the Bruins lost Bobby Orr. But, unlike Orr, Bourque has never known the thrill of a Stanley Cup championship.

Perhaps *Hockey News* editor Steve Dryden said it best:"He may be the closest thing to a perfect defenseman the NHL has ever seen — although I can't decide if that makes him better than Bobby Orr."

Hockey commentator Harry Neale marvels at the 37-year-old's stamina. When told Bourque logged an average of 30 minutes per game, and saw more ice in 1997–98 (2,462 minutes), than any other player, Neale quipped, "The guy's a horse. I'm surprised they don't have some apples and some oats on the Bruin bench to feed him when he comes off the ice."

Bourque tied Coffey's record of 385 goals.

"Scoring that many goals impresses even me," Bourque said, "because defense has always been my main priority."

Kasper Versus Gretzky

N 1981–82, defensive forward Steve Kasper of the Bruins became the first NHL player other than Montreal's Bob Gainey to capture the Frank J. Selke Trophy (Gainey was runner-up). The award, first presented in 1978 to "the forward who excels in the defensive aspects of the game," had been swept up by Gainey for four straight years. On the day the awards were presented in Montreal, Kasper's home city, he got a chance to talk to Wayne Gretzky, who was coming off a 92-goal season (still an NHL record).

"Wayne came up to me and said, 'Congratulations, Steve.' It's the first time I ever talked to him or shook his hand. I didn't know what to expect from Wayne because I stuck to him like glue on the ice. I know it's one reason I was considered for the Selke Award."

When asked how he responded to Gretzky, Kasper replied, "I said the obvious. 'Congratulations, Wayne.' I mean the guy won a lot of hardware, didn't he?"

What Kasper may not have realized is that Gretzky might have become hockey's first 100-goal scorer if it hadn't been for the young Bruin's amazing ability to keep the Great One off the scoresheet. In a season when two, three, or four goals in a game were commonplace for Gretzky, Kasper allowed him just one goal total in the three games they played against each other.

Gretzky was quick to credit Kasper for his diligent checking: "The stats show that he's done the best job against me and stats don't lie," Gretzky said. "In the past two seasons I have 2 goals and 6 assists against the Bruins. I guess I'll have to try something new the next time Steve and I are on the ice together."

Kasper said of the game's top goal scorer, "You can't take risks and you can't take cheap penalties when you're checking Gretzky. You've got to keep yourself near him but not all over him. If you get in his way, and he doesn't have the puck, they'll call you for interference. I like shadowing him — if I'm successful. But he's such a great player you know he can break a game wide open at any time."

Injuries slowed Kasper for the two seasons following his Selke Award year and he never won the trophy again. He came back with 20 goals and 50 points in 1986–87 and 26 goals and 70 points a year later. He was traded to the Kings in January 1989 for Bobby Carpenter, a center who gave the Bruins two 25-goal seasons before moving on to Philadelphia and, finally, Tampa Bay.

The Irascible Irishman

ONE of the most colorful players ever to wear a Bruins jersey during the seventies and eighties was Terry O'Reilly. With an Irish name and a hellbent style of play (along with some scoring talent) O'Reilly became an overnight hometown favorite. The fans named him "Taz," after Tasmanian Devil, a cartoon character who trampled everything in its path.

Off the ice, O'Reilly displayed a quiet, caring, intellectual side. He volunteered for charity work in the community. He loved good books and collecting antiques. Family was important to him.

When Don Cherry's son Tim underwent a kidney transplant, O'Reilly was one of the first of several Bruins to donate blood.

On the ice, he was Cherry's kind of player, skating recklessly up and down the wing, crashing and bashing anyone who dared to get in his path. If an altercation broke out, he never backed down. When challenged, he often let his opponent take the first shot. Or he'd let them get set to take it. Cherry would shake his head and say, "O'Reilly, you're too nice to be known as a tough guy."

His style of play sometimes landed him in trouble. During the seventh and deciding game in the 1982 Conference semi-finals against Quebec, he was ejected from the game for punching a referee. The Bruins lost the game and the series. After a review of the tapes, O'Reilly was suspended for the first ten games of the following season by NHL executive vice-president Brian O'Neill.

In a game against Minnesota on October 26, 1977, O'Reilly received a minor penalty for tripping. He appeared to purposely bump into referee Dennis Morel to argue the call. Then he threw his gloves at the official in disgust and skated off the ice. Morel threw him out of the game and the league followed up with a three-game suspension.

In the 1977–78 season, O'Reilly became the first player in NHL history to finish among the top ten scorers and collect more than 200 penalty minutes. Only two other players have matched his feat — Kevin Stevens in 1991–92 and Brendan Shanahan in 1993–94.

During his career, he amassed 606 points (204 goals, 402 assists) and a staggering 2,095 minutes in penalties in 891 regular season games — still a club record. He ranks eighth overall among Boston's all-time point leaders in regular season play. As you might expect, he's number one on the list of most penalized Bruins.

In 1986, after his playing career ended, O'Reilly was invited to coach the Bruins, and he held the position for three seasons. He finished with a respectable record of 115 wins, 86 losses, and 26 ties in 227 regular season games.

Nobody calls him Taz anymore. The name only seemed fitting when he had skates on his feet and a piece of lumber in his hands.

Sinden Should Have Kept Fergus

TOM Fergus was an unlikely candidate for NHL play. As an aspiring teenage player he was cut from a Junior B team in Brantford, Ontario, and sent to a Junior D team in nearby St. George. "Too small," was the verdict of the Brantford coach.

"And he was right, too," Fergus recalls. "Even in Junior D I was the smallest guy on the team. Then I grew about a foot in one season. Suddenly I was a six-footer and I was recruited by the Peterborough Petes Junior A club. That's where I was in 1980 when the Bruins found me and drafted me. I don't know what they saw in me. I scored only 8 goals in my first year with the Petes."

The Bruins grabbed Fergus with the 60th pick that year. He didn't stop growing until he was 6'3" and 210 pounds. And by then he'd developed one of the best wrist shots the Bruin scouts had ever seen.

"The kids scored 43 goals in his final year with the Petes," said veteran Jean Ratelle. "And when he made it with [the Bruins], it was partly because he could drill that puck like, none of the other rookies in the league."

Fergus scored 15, 28, 25, and 30 goals in his first four seasons as a Bruin. Ratelle raved about Fergus's skating, passing, and playmaking. He also mentioned Fergus's name in the same breath as Dale Hawerchuk, Denis Savard, and Barry Pederson, the Bruins' number one draft choice in 1980.

Pederson compiled 44 goals and 92 points to overshadow Fergus during the 1981–82 season, but both youngsters had made an effortless leap to the pros and were both expected to wear Boston jerseys for the next decade, and possibly beyond.

But it was not to be. In 1985, Harry Sinden thought he had a chance to outsmart Toronto in a deal. He sent Fergus to the

Leafs in return for Billy Derlago. But Derlago, who'd enjoyed one 40-goal and three 30-plus goal seasons as a Leaf, was sliding downhill fast. He scored a mere 5 goals as a Bruin in 39 games, and when Sinden had seen enough, he passed him along to Winnipeg in return for Wade Campbell, a plodding defenseman who played less than 30 games as a Bruin over the next three seasons.

Sinden should have kept Fergus — or received more for him than Derlago. Fergus had five solid years in Toronto before injuries began to take their toll.

Bruins Score Impossible Record

TWO goals in two seconds. Doesn't seem possible, does it? Especially in the NHL.

But hockey is full of surprises, and on December 19, 1987, the Bruins and the St. Louis Blues combined to set the record for the quickest two goals in hockey history.

The Bruins were trailing the Blues 6–4 in the last minute of play. Then, with ten seconds left on the clock and goalie Doug Keans on the Boston bench, Ken Linseman scored for Boston. The Bruins trailed by one goal.

The ensuing faceoff was won by the Blues' Doug Gilmour. He whacked the puck hard down the ice and straight into the empty Boston cage. A mere two seconds had elapsed from the time of Linseman's goal.

The Bruins may have lost the game 7–5, but Linseman and Gilmour established a mark that lives on in the NHL record books.

Bruins Part of
Meadowlands Fiasco

WHEN the Boston Bruins and the New Jersey Devils met in the Wales Conference finals in 1988, there were more heated exchanges off the ice than on it.

Game Three ended on a shocking note, with Devils coach Jim Schoenfeld blistering referee Don Koharski with a verbal attack in a corridor. Some say he pushed Koharski. Among other things, Schoenfeld said the referee was "full of shit." He called Koharski "a fat pig" and suggested he "eat another donut." For his outburst Schoenfeld was suspended, a decision that infuriated his team's owners.

Between games, the Devils served the league with a restraining order signed by a judge from a New Jersey court, a ruling that allowed Schoenfeld to continue coaching. NHL officials were flabbergasted. No member club had ever defied a suspension before by running to the courts for help.

The Devils' actions triggered a wildcat strike by the game officials prior to Game Four. The walkout was led by veteran referee Dave Newell, who demanded a guarantee of safer working conditions. When it was not forthcoming, the officials struck.

NHL bigwigs searched frantically for substitute officials to work Game Four. The best they could do was to recruit 52-year-old part-time referee Paul McInnis, and linesmen Vin Godleski, 51, and Jim Sullivan, 50. The crowd hooted when they stepped on the ice because only McInnis wore a standard referee's shirt. The two linesmen wore yellow practice jerseys, green pants, and borrowed skates.

The game was played without any major incidents. McInnis survived his afternoon without controversy and even appeared on *Good Morning, America* the next morning.

Boston general manager Harry Sinden observed, with a trace

of sarcasm, "The difference between those officials, three old guys we pulled from the stands, and our regular guys was marginal."

Further complicating the events of the day was the strange disappearance of NHL president John Ziegler. He was nowhere to be found. Later, a league employee, requesting anonymity, hinted that he was on a golfing vacation in the Carolinas.

Even today, a slimmed-down Don Koharski gets kidded about his penchant for donuts. He told me once, "The morning after the Schoenfeld outburst, my wife left our home in Burlington, Ontario, to go shopping. Without thinking, she went into a Tim Hortons donut shop, one she visited regularly. She ordered a dozen to go. For a minute, she couldn't understand why all the guys and girls behind the counter were laughing. They were obviously hockey fans. In the movie *Wayne's World*, the policeman frequently seen at "Stan Mikita's Donuts" was named Officer Koharski!

The Bruins won that series over the Devils in seven games, but they ran into the powerful Edmonton Oilers in the Stanley Cup finals and were swept aside in four games. The Oilers suffered only two losses in 19 playoff games that year and Wayne Gretzky soared to new heights with a record 43 points.

Stardom Was Imminent for Leveille

THE 1982–83 NHL season was nicely under way. The Bruins were in Vancouver for a Saturday, October 23, game with the Canucks. At breakfast some of the Bruins talked about a Montreal kid who had cracked the lineup and already had made quite an impact — 19-year-old Normand Leveille. Terry O'Reilly said, "He's going to be very good. Hell, he's going to be better than Yvan Cournoyer of the Canadiens."

In the game that night, Leveille took a hard first-period check into the boards from Marc Crawford of the Canucks. But he bounced right up and darted back into the play.

During the first intermission, Boston assistant coach Jean Ratelle was surprised when Leveille approached him in the dressing room. "Jean, something's wrong. I feel very dizzy," he told Ratelle.

Suspecting a concussion, Ratelle led the rookie into the Bruins' medical room, where he was examined by Jimmy Kausek, the team's physical therapist. "I told him to lie down and he didn't respond," Kausek recalls. "Then I asked him to squeeze my hand and he didn't respond. He had a glazed look and he didn't seem to have any motor control on his right side. I told someone to get a doctor."

Dr. Ross Davidson, the Vancouver team doctor, was sought. He took one look at Leveille and said, "Get this boy to a hospital." He summoned an ambulance.

"The young man didn't look good at all," the doctor said. "He was conscious for a few minutes in the ambulance but once we reached the hospital he deteriorated very quickly."

Leveille was wheeled straight into the operating room. Working quickly, two neurosurgeons cut a hole an inch square in Leveille's skull. They attempted to repair the damage done by a sudden flow of blood to the brain. It was determined that a blood vessel, defective since birth but undetectable until that moment, had ruptured, spilling blood throughout the delicate tissues inside the skill.

"It could have been triggered by the hit by Crawford," said Dr. Davidson. "Then again, it could have happened from something as simple as a sneeze. It could have happened anytime. It was congenital. I think we can say young Leveille will never play hockey again."

Dr. Davidson's prediction was on the mark. Leveille's promising career was snuffed out and his young life came perilously close to an end. He never did play hockey again. But he did skate again at the Boston Garden.

On September 26, 1995, 14,448 teary-eyed fans said goodbye to the Boston Garden in a 3–0 exhibition win over Montreal.

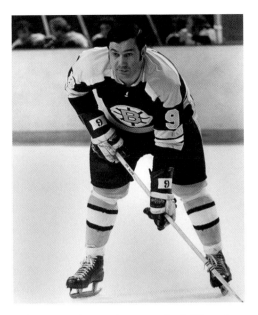

Johnny Bucyk scored a career-high 51 goals for Boston in 1970–71 when he was 35 years old. He was inducted into the Hockey Hall of Fame in 1981. — Robert B. Shaver

Don Cherry, who played only one game for the Bruins, coached Boston for five seasons and was named NHL coach of the year in 1976. — Hockey Hall of Fame

During the 1960s and '70s Gerry Cheevers was possibly the best clutch goaltender in the NHL. He led the Bruins to Stanley Cups in 1970 and 1972. — Hockey Hall of Fame

In May 1967, Phil Esposito was the central figure in a major deal between the Bruins and the Blackhawks. In Boston, he combined with Bobby Orr to rewrite the NHL record book.
— Hockey Hall of Fame

Rugged Terry O'Reilly served over 2,000 penalty minutes during his 891-game career with the Bruins. — Hockey Hall of Fame

Harry Sinden has been the general manager of the Bruins since 1972–73 and has served as club president since 1989–90. He is a Lester Patrick Award winner and was named to the Hall of Fame in 1983.
— Hockey Hall of Fame

Craig MacTavish played for the Bruins for most of five seasons. His conviction for vehicular manslaughter interrupted his career and changed his life.
— Hockey Hall of Fame

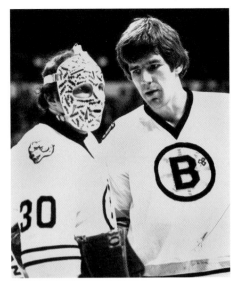

Boston's Mike Milbury was one of the first to question the decisions and policies of former NHLPA executive director Alan Eagleson. Milbury played with the Bruins from 1976 to 1987. — Hockey Hall of Fame

Gerry Cheevers, wearing his famous mask, and Terry O'Reilly. Both went on to coach the Bruins following their playing careers. — Hockey Hall of Fame

Derek Sanderson became hockey's highest-paid player when he jumped from the Bruins to the Philadelphia Blazers of the WHA in 1972. — Robert B. Shaver

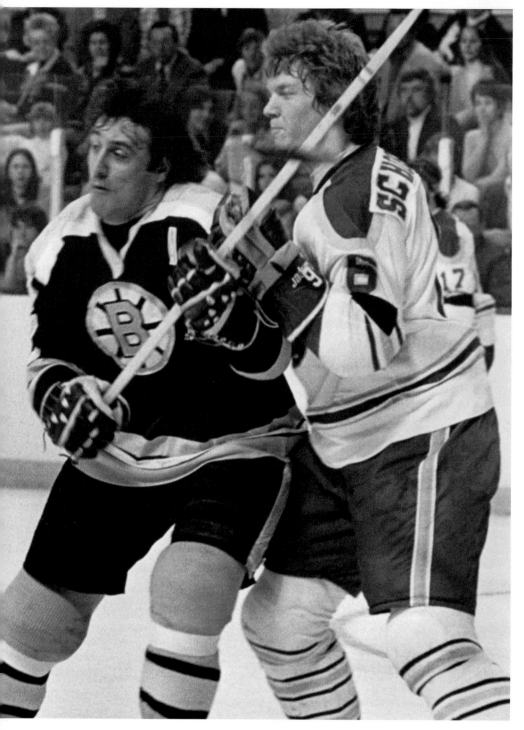

Phil Esposito, held in check here by Buffalo's Jim Schoenfeld, set NHL records of 76 goals and 152 points in 1970–71. Both marks were eclipsed by Wayne Gretzky a decade later. — Robert B. Shaver

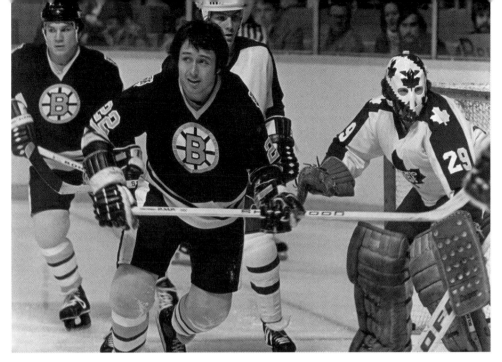

Former Ranger star Brad Park joined the Bruins as part of a controversial deal in November 1975. He was runner-up to Bobby Orr for the Norris Trophy four times in a five-year span. — Robert B. Shaver

Goaltender Ross Brooks, who joined the Bruins as a 35-year-old rookie in 1972–73, went on to play the best hockey of his life and finished his three-season career with a 37–7–6 record. — Hockey Hall of Fame

Dave Forbes was charged with aggravated assault after an altercation with Minnesota's Henry Boucha in 1975. His trial ended in a hung jury and he was freed. A follow-up civil suit against Forbes resulted in a $1.3-million settlement. — Hockey Hall of Fame

Acquired from the Rangers in a deal for Ken Hodge in 1976, Rick Middleton scored over 400 goals as a Bruin.
— Hockey Hall of Fame

For 15 seasons, the gritty, take-no-prisoners approach embodied by Wayne Cashman was the spirit of the Big Bad Bruins.
— Hockey Hall of Fame

A glittering star for 21 seasons, Boston's Ray Bourque holds club records for games played and points. — Hockey Hall of Fame

Cam Neely established himself as the NHL's top power forward in the late 1980s. His brilliant career was cut short by a serious knee injury. — Robert B. Shaver

In 1998–99, goalie Byron Dafoe faced 1,800 shots, the most recorded in Bruins' history, and had a save percentage of .926, second only to Buffalo's Hasek.
— Hockey Hall of Fame

Acquired from the Kings (with Byron Dafoe) in 1997, Dmitri Khristich was the Bruins' leading goal scorer in 1998–99 with 29 goals.   — Hockey Hall of Fame

Only two 17-year-olds have been drafted number one overall in the NHL — Boston's Joe Thornton (in 1997) and Pierre Turgeon (selected by Buffalo in 1987).
— Hockey Hall of Fame

As a 15-year-old, Russian-born Sergei Samsonov's coach said he was better than Gretzky at the same age. In 1998, Samsonov became the seventh Bruin to win the Calder Trophy.
— Hockey Hall of Fame

Boston acquired Anson Carter in a trade with Washington in 1997. In 1998–99 he enjoyed a career season with 24 goals in 55 games — not bad for a player who was drafted 220th overall in 1992. — Hockey Hall of Fame

In 86 games over parts of four seasons with Washington, Jason Allison scored a mere seven goals. He scored 33 goals in his first full season in Boston and led the team in scoring with 83 points.
— Hockey Hall of Fame

Although he's often overshadowed by Ray Bourque, Kyle McLaren gives the Bruins strong leadership on defense.
— Hockey Hall of Fame

In Pat Burns' first season with Boston (1997–98), the Bruins improved by a remarkable 30 points. He's the only man to win the Adams Trophy as coach of the year with three different clubs.
— Hockey Hall of Fame

Thunderous ovations poured down on former stars Bobby Orr, Johnny Bucyk, Terry O'Reilly, Stan Jonathon, Gerry Cheevers, and former coach Don Cherry. Then they gasped in disbelief as Normand Leveille's name was called to join the proud alumni on the ice. On shaky legs and holding a cane instead of a hockey stick, Leveille touched his skates to the ice as the cheering crowd stood and applauded. With the help of Ray Bourque, Leveille glided slowly to center ice where a special chair was hastily set up for him. Permanent damage from the cerebral hemorrhage that crippled him nearly thirteen years before slowed him down, but there was no doubting the strength of his heart. He made it to the chair. He was where he'd longed to be and he'd covered the distance on skates.

Bobby Orr said, "I was so excited for him. Normand has so much courage. To me, it was the highlight of the evening."

MacTavish Gets a Second Chance

I T was the worst day of his life, a day so horrible, so depressing, so filled with guilt and self-condemnation, he vowed that it would also be the first day of a new life, a better life.

Craig MacTavish, a 25-year-old Boston Bruin forward, was going to jail.

In May 1984, in Salem, Massachusetts, superior court judge Andrew Linscott sentenced MacTavish to one year in prison. Earlier, MacTavish had pleaded guilty to vehicular homicide.

Fighting to hold back tears of remorse, MacTavish told the courtroom, including the parents of the young victim, that he had made a "big, big mistake."

MacTavish had been drinking at the Golden Banana Club

prior to the accident. Staff at the club testified they had stopped serving him drinks because he'd been drunk and loud.

MacTavish drove off in his car, and a few minutes later, on Route 1 in Peabody, Massachusetts, he ploughed into the rear end of a Pinto driven by Kim Radley, a young housewife from Newfield, Maine. Police estimated MacTavish was travelling between 60 and 85 miles per hour when he struck the young woman's car, knocking it into a nearby parking lot, where it flipped on its side. Radley was critically injured and later died.

At first, MacTavish denied charges of operating a vehicle under the influence of alcohol, driving to endanger, vehicular homicide, and driving without a licence. Later, he changed his plea to guilty and said, "After witnessing my own family's pain over the incident, I can only imagine the pain suffered by the Radley family."

The victim's husband, Michael, was said to be too grief-stricken to attend the trial. Her father, Ronalde Foote, told the court, "My daughter would want this young man to pick up the pieces a lot wiser and make something of himself."

MacTavish vowed to put his life back together when he was freed from prison. The Boston Bruins' management said it would make every effort to assist MacTavish in renewing his hockey career once he fulfilled his obligation to society. MacTavish served his time, was out of hockey for a year, and returned to the NHL in 1985–86. But not with the Bruins.

Harry Sinden figured the pressure on MacTavish in Boston would be unbearable under the circumstances, and generously allowed him to sign with the Edmonton Oilers as a free agent.

MacTavish played nine years in Edmonton, where he celebrated three Stanley Cup triumphs. He was traded to the Rangers in time to help them capture the 1994 Cup, moved on to the Flyers for a couple of seasons, and wound up his career in St. Louis.

MacTavish will never forget those dark days when he was incarcerated and out of hockey in 1984 and 1985. He can never erase completely from his thoughts those reckless few minutes that brought tragedy to so many.

Overnight he became more serious about life, more responsible, more mature. He spoke to young people about the hazards of drinking and driving. He became, he says, a much better person.

"I was very fortunate that Glen Sather gave me a second chance. There was a time when I didn't think I'd get one — or even deserved one."

Summer of '86

A lot of startling events took place in hockey in the summer of '86.

Former Bruin Brad Park was fired as coach of the Red Wings. The Wings were counting on Michigan State grad Joe Murphy, the first college player to be drafted Number One overall, to move them up in the standings. George Pelawa, Calgary's first draft choice, was killed in a car accident in Bemidji, Minnesota. Dan Maloney quit as coach of the Leafs and signed on with John Ferguson's Winnipeg Jets, while coach John Brophy brought his tough guy act to Maple Leaf Gardens. Borje Salming admitted he'd tried cocaine and was suspended for eight regular-season games. Phil Esposito took over as general manager of the Rangers and was surprised to hear Barry Beck, his star defenseman, say he'd retire from hockey before he'd play for coach Ted Sator. Early in the new season, Wayne Gretzky scored a hat trick against the Bruins, the thirty-eighth of his career.

Almost overlooked in all of this shifting of hockey bodies was a deal consummated on June 6 between Boston and Vancouver. The Bruins gave up Barry Pederson in return for Cam Neely and a first-round draft choice in 1987 (who turned out to be Glen Wesley).

Pederson played for another six seasons, scoring 75 goals. Neely blossomed as a Bruin and scored 344 goals in the next ten seasons. The addition of Wesley made the deal one of the best in Boston history. No wonder then, when Neely was forced to retire on September 1996, due to an ailing hip, there was sadness throughout New England. Bruin fans literally adored the hard-nosed right winger for his scoring touch and his devastating body checks.

Neely, 31, left the game with 395 goals and 299 assists. He scored 50 or more goals in a season three times and in 1994–95 he reached the 50-goal plateau in his forty-fourth game, becoming the third-fastest player to reach the mark.

"Replace him? You can't replace a Neely," said Adam Oates, who assisted on many of Neely's goals during their time in Boston together. "There just aren't that many 50- to 60-goal scorers around."

In his prime, he was the NHL's top power forward. His crashing, go-for-the-net style would have fit right in with the Big Bad Bruins of Sanderson, Cashman, Bucyk, and Orr.

"Bobby and I talked about it often," Sanderson once said. "Neely is the one guy who could have played with us."

The trade for Neely continues to have repercussions. Glen Wesley, whom the Bruins drafted with the pick they received in the deal, served the Bruins well through 537 games. When Wesley opted for free agency, Harry Sinden traded him to Hartford for three first-round draft picks. Two of these draft choices turned out to be Kyle MacLaren and Sergei Samsonov. It was another sweet deal for Sinden.

Neely tried a comeback in 1998, his passion for the game undiminished after two seasons on the sidelines. But the hip wouldn't cooperate and he stepped aside for a second time. His name lives on in the establishment of Neely House, a haven for families who stand vigil while their dear ones undergo treatment for cancer, a disease that claimed both of Neely's parents.

Bruins Couldn't Give Courtnall Away

GEOFF Courtnall had been a big scorer in junior hockey. With Victoria in 1982–83 he scored 41 goals and collected 114 points.

When the Bruins signed him as a free agent in July 1983, they thought they'd landed someone special. But after a decent 12-game season as a rookie in 1984–85, Courtnall fell into a terrible slump in his second year. It was a classic case of the sophomore jinx.

In December 1985, Harry Sinden had seen enough. He placed Courtnall on waivers, and the 20 other clubs in the NHL showed no interest, even though many of them were desperate for help.

"He had a reputation as a streaky player," said Sinden. "One minute I was ready to pack him in, the next I was ready to give him a raise."

Then, to Sinden's amazement, Courtnall recovered to score 21 goals. "He started to come through at the perfect time. If he hadn't, he would have been in the minors."

Courtnall fell back to 13 goals the following season, but produced 32 goals for the Bruins by March 8, 1988. That was the day Sinden traded him to Edmonton.

The player he couldn't give away a few months earlier was now coveted by the Oilers. In return for Courtnall, goalie Bill Ranford, and future considerations, Sinden picked up goalie Andy Moog, who gave the Bruins solid netminding for the next five seasons.

Sinden Sizzles over Vicious Check by Chelios

D URING a game between the Bruins and the Canadiens at the Forum in 1986–87, Montreal defenseman Chris Chelios smashed Boston's Rick Middleton into the boards, knocking him unconscious. Middleton was carried off on a stretcher and an early diagnosis indicated he may have suffered a fractured skull. Fortunately, Middleton did not suffer a fracture, though he did suffer a concussion.

Boston general manager Harry Sinden was livid when no penalty was called on Chelios. Between periods, he stormed into the officials' dressing room and called referee Kerry Fraser either a liar or a cheat.

"I told Fraser it's one of two things," Sinden told reporters. "Either he was lying because he didn't see it or he was a cheat because he saw it but didn't call it."

And what did Fraser say? "Ha! He said it was a legal check."

Because of Sinden's invasion of the officials' sanctum, the Bruins were assessed an unsportsmanlike conduct penalty. Later, Sinden was fined $2,000 for his accusations against Fraser.

Hawgood Scores
First Playoff Goal
in Phantom Game

BRUIN Greg Hawgood scored his first playoff goal and Rick Middleton collected his 100th career playoff point in a game that was never finished and never really existed.

On the night of May 24, 1988, the lights went out at the Boston Garden and a playoff game had to be abandoned, driving a huge spike into the Bruins' Stanley Cup hopes. It's an amazing little slice of Stanley Cup lore.

The Bruins that playoff season battled their way past Buffalo in six games, Montreal in five, and New Jersey in seven to win the Wales Conference championship. Incidentally, the last time the Bruins had ousted Montreal in a playoff series was in 1943, a year before the red line was introduced to hockey.

After the Bruins triumphed over the Devils, the only obstacle standing between them and the Stanley Cup was the cocky Edmonton Oilers, winners of three Stanley Cups since dethroning the Islander dynasty in 1984.

The Oilers had breezed past Detroit in the Campbell Conference finals, four games to one. Half a dozen Red Wings, sharing a "what's-the-use" attitude when it came to playing against the Oilers, were caught drinking and breaking curfew on the eve of Game Five. Coach Jacques Demers was furious and threatened heavy fines and possible trades involving the party-lovers. Owner Mike Ilitch, prepared to hand out thousands of dollars in bonus cheques to his players, decided not to give a dime to the curfew breakers.

The Cup final opened in Edmonton, with the Oilers capturing Games One and Two by 2–1 and 4–2 scores. Back in Boston the Oilers won again, 6–3. In Game Four, the Bruins played with great intensity and led 3–2 in the second period. Late in the frame, Craig Simpson of the Oilers beat goaltender Andy Moog to tie the score. Just as play was about to resume, the lights went out at the Boston Garden.

The old arena remained in total darkness for a few minutes. Then an emergency generator kicked in, but it could not deliver enough current or candlepower to light up a playoff game. The heat, humidity, and antiquated equipment were blamed for the electrical failure.

John Ziegler huddled with other officials and invoked NHL by-law (27.12c), which states: "If for any cause beyond the control of the clubs a playoff game should be unfinished, such game shall be replayed in its entirety at the end of the series if necessary and it shall be replayed in the rink in which the unfinished game occurred."

All parties, including Harry Sinden, went along with the Ziegler decision.

"But what about the game stats? What about Hawgood's first playoff goal?

Ziegler announced that the game stats would remain valid, even though the game might never be replayed. And even if it was replayed, all goals and assists from the unfinished game would still count.

As it turned out, the game was not replayed. The teams flew off to Edmonton where the Oilers completed a series sweep two nights later, winning Game Four (some might say Game Five) by a 6–3 score.

Years from now, when Greg Hawgood's grandchildren ask him if he ever scored a goal in the Stanley Cup playoffs (he scored two in 42 games), he will laugh and say, "Kids, you're not going to believe this, but . . ."

The Fascinating Nineties

Neely's Unwashed Mouthpiece Fetches a Fortune

CAN you imagine paying $665 for a hockey star's dirty old mouthpiece? A 38-year-old woman, an attorney from the suburb of Arlington, Massachusetts, named Paula Mattaliano, did in September 1996. It was the day they auctioned off thousands of items after the closing of the Boston Garden.

What did she do with it? The first thing she did was pop it in her mouth and sink her teeth into it. Her friends' reaction? "Gross! How could you, Paula?"

Paula shrugged. "No big deal," she said. "We've all French-kissed people, haven't we? A French kiss is more germ-filled than a little piece of plastic."

Paula was among the 4,000 fans who turned out to bid enthusiastically on everything from Stanley Cup banners to the Garden scoreboard. She was thrilled to be the winning bidder on a small personal item belonging to her favorite Bruin, even if the price she paid raised a few eyebrows.

"I have loved the Bruins since I was a fetus," Paula said, popping the mouthpiece out to make certain her message was clear. "It took ten years in my heart and soul to replace Bobby Orr and Cam Neely did that."

Other items auctioned off included the Boston Garden Zamboni ($15,000), the scoreboard ($44,000), the original architectural plans for the building ($10,000), the 1970 Stanley Cup banner ($8,000), and Phil Esposito's stall from the Bruin dressing room ($2,500).

A jersey worn by Bobby Orr from his Junior days in Oshawa was the only item that did not sell. It carried a minimum bid of $10,000 and the bidding stopped at $8,000.

The Bruins donated all proceeds to charity.

Drafted Dead Last

C'MON. Trading your 245th draft choice to a team for their 246th? It doesn't make sense. But to the Boston Bruins it did. At the 1997 Entry Draft in Pittsburgh, the Bruins, drafting first overall, snared center Joe Thornton, supposedly a blue-chip prospect. Hours later, in the ninth and final round, the Bruins felt an urge to make the final selection as well. So they traded the 245th pick to Colorado for the 246th, bottom-of-the barrel selection. The Bruins claimed left winger Jay Henderson from the Edmonton Ice of the Western league. Their day's work done, and stifling yawns, everybody got up and went home.

Incredibly, a few months later, Henderson actually showed up on the Bruins' roster, suiting up for a game on October 28 against Montreal. The kid who'd scored 49 goals for the Ice a year earlier was ecstatic, even though he played in only three games after that. "How many kids drafted dead last make it to the NHL?" he asked. Henderson went from the bottom of the barrel to the top of the heap!

Shooting in Vain

"WE took 73 shots on the guy and at least half of them were quality shots," said Ray Bourque after a game at the Boston Garden on March 21, 1991. "The man was unbelievable. Why, I took a record 19 shots myself."

Bourque was lavish in his praise for Quebec Nordique netminder Ron Tugnutt, who stopped 70 shots in the game and was delighted to skate off with a 3–3 tie.

Half a century earlier, the Bruins had taken a record 83 shots in a game, against Chicago's Sam LoPresti on another March night in 1941. But they'd won that match 3–2.

Tugnutt left the Bruins shaking their heads in frustration as the shots piled up and one brilliant save followed another. He reserved his best effort for the overtime frame. With eight seconds left on the clock, the puck came to Bourque, who saw nothing but net. He blasted a slapshot, certain it was the winning goal. But Tugnutt's glove shot out and snared the rubber.

"I never saw that one," Tugnutt would say later, grinning. "I just stuck the glove out and there it was."

At the final whistle, the Bruins congratulated Tugnutt as he skated off, his ordeal over. Cam Neely was so impressed he waved for a spotlight to shine down on the courageous goalie. "Take a bow, take a bow," Neely urged him.

But Tugnutt declined. "That was nice, to be congratulated by the Bruins," Tugnutt told reporters. "You don't often see that in hockey — except after a team loses a playoff series. Late in the game I could see the Bruins shaking their heads and laughing. Then I had to turn away or I would have started laughing, too."

"A lot of those shots were bullets," Harry Sinden said. "There weren't many easy ones."

"He deserved all three stars," added Bourque.

Bring Your Wallet
to the FleetCenter

KEVIN Dupont, writing in *The Hockey News*, wasn't as enthralled with the opening of the FleetCenter as he might have been. He says going to the FleetCenter is no longer just a night of hockey. It is hockey fit into a wining and dining experience. And oh, if you're coming, Kevin suggests, remember to bring your wallet (an all-beef hot dog and small Coke costs $6). "They weren't giving out goodies at the Garden, either, but gouging is a major penalty at every concession stand in the new place."

Kevin's other observations on the new building follow:

The FleetCenter in no way mirrors the building it replaced. Is that all bad? No. Anyone who ever had the distinct pleasure of purchasing one of the Garden's horrendous obstructed-view seats, and paid the chiropractor's bill that came with it, will have to embrace the Bruins' new home.

The new arena is clean. It is comfortable. It is everything the Baby Boomer generation demands: cushy seats, loads of leg room, a TV monitor at every turn (in excess of 500 throughout the building), and restaurants (one with a champagne and caviar bar).

High prices aren't the Fleet's biggest surprise. It took $160 million to build the place. It is the house Jeremy Jacobs built and he knows the price tolerance of the Boston sporting public. We pay. He profits. For twenty-plus years now, none with a Bruins' Stanley Cup, it has been a proven championship formula.

The Fleet is a virtual cookie-cutter knockoff of every new sports arena. Upper bowl. Lower bowl. Drop by your local drug store today and pick up the blueprints (free with your purchase of an NHL mug).

So what? So nothing, except we here in Boston like to believe we are something special, that the ivy-covered walls of Harvard and the claustrophobic Green Monster of Fenway Park, even the tourist-trap Cheers bar, distinguish us.

Bostonians like to think they are special. We call our town the Hub, believing quite humbly, we are the hub of the universe. Because of this attitude, out-of-towners find us to be smug and snobby. Those hicks. They just don't recognize civic pride when they see it.

With just a slight brush of ingenuity, someone could have taken the Camden Yards approach to the Fleet and put some old-world touches to the place. Boston is a town of brick and brownstone. Perhaps the facades of the balconies — sacred signage positions, I know — could have been dressed up with brick to lend the building a Back Bay appeal. The old Chicago Stadium had its powerful pipe organ as its signature. Perhaps a booming Baldwin would have been enough to make Boston better.

What we have here is a fabulous new place to go, to eat, to be merry in the way we define merry in the 1990s, and probably will define merry well into the next millennium.

Lost in it all, though, is something more than we expected. Every old building put to rest surrenders its history and a city mourns the passing of those times when the building is razed. But when the new building is put up without the slightest sense of the city in which it represents, it has missed the point before the first goal has been scored.

Boston, same as it ever was, but now the same as virtually everywhere else. Our Town has become Our Town.

Bruins Welcome
Allison and Khristich

ONLY two Bruin forwards — Dmitri Khistich and Jason Allison — topped 70 points in 1998–99. Both young sharpshooters arrived in Boston by trades made by the astute Harry Sinden.

In 1993, Allison, the Canadian major junior player of the year in 1994, was drafted 17th overall by Washington, where he struggled for a couple of seasons trying to ignite his NHL career. On March 1, 1997, he became part of a memorable six-player trade with Boston. The Bruins acquired Allison, forward Anson Carter, goalie Jim Carey (winner of the Vezina Trophy the previous season), and a third-round draft choice in return for goalie Bill Ranford, playmaker Adam Oates (who had slipped to 70 points after four 100-plus point seasons), and Rick Tocchet, who was beginning to show his years.

"The trade gave me new hope and a fresh start," said Allison. "The Bruins gave me a chance to show my stuff and there was a big leap in confidence." Allison scored 33 goals — 8 of them game winners — and 83 points in his first full season to lead the Bruins in points. He followed up with 23–53–76 totals to lead the Bruins in points in 1998–99. Anston Carter was a pleasant surprise, too, scoring 8 goals in 19 games to close out the 1996–97 season, 16 goals in his second year as a Bruin, and 24 goals in 1998–99.

However, goalie Jim Carey, clutching a huge contract, was a huge disappointment. He couldn't beat out Byron Dafoe for the Bruin goaltending job and wound up in Providence. In March 1999, his contract was bought out by the club and he signed with St. Louis as a free agent.

Adam Oates, meanwhile, enjoyed a good season in Washington in 1997–98 (76 points) and followed up with 54 points in

1998–99, despite missing several games because of injury. Ranford played back-up to Olaf Kolzig in Washington. Kolzig played when it counted, performing brilliantly in all 21 playoff games, taking the Caps to the 1998 Cup finals against Detroit. At the trade deadline in March 1999, Ranford ended up with Detroit.

Dmitri Khristich, as well as Dafoe, had once been abandoned by the Capitals, too. In 1995, the Caps dealt the pair to Los Angeles in return for the King's first-round draft choice (Alexander Volchkov) and a fourth rounder (Justin Davis).

After two seasons with the Kings, Khristich and Dafoe were on the move again, to Boston. Harry Sinden must have felt like a cat with a canary in his mouth when the Kings agreed to take Sandy Moger, Jozef Stumpel, and a fourth-round draft choice for the pair. In 1998–99 Khristich (29–42–71) battled Allison for the team scoring title (he came second) while Dafoe's goals-against average (1.99 in 68 games) was third best in the NHL.

When the Capitals fell from Stanley Cup finalists to finishing out of the playoffs the following seasons, fans wondered how they might have fared if they'd had the foresight to keep Khristich, Dafoe, Allison, and Carter.

When the Sabres bumped the Bruins out of the playoffs in 1999, Allison and Khristich were on the receiving end of a blast from Sinden.

"We paid these guys a lot of money and I don't think it helped them," Sinden growled. "Allison wasn't the player he was last year. He wasn't the player he should have been against Buffalo. I paid him. If you want it and you get it, then earn it, baby, earn it. As for Khristich, he was a total disappointment [against Buffalo]. All he did was give the puck to the other team."

Bruins' Last-Minute Collapse

THE Bruins who played against the Dallas Stars on the night of October 14, 1995, have never forgotten the ending to that game. They'd like to, but they can't. Especially Boston netminder Craig Billington, who was coasting to victory when . . . well, let's start at the beginning and recap the scoring.

Cam Neely had a big first period, scoring his fifth and sixth goals of the new season, and the Bruins grabbed a 2–1 lead. Todd Elik and Stephen Heinze added second-period goals, sandwiched around one by Dallas, and the Bruins held a comfortable 4–2 lead heading into the final frame.

Early in the third period, Guy Carbonneau tallied for the Stars, but Elik scored his second of the night at 5:44 to restore the Bruins' two-goal margin.

Billington heard the PA announcer tell the crowd, "This is the final minute of play in the period." Perhaps he looked up at the clock to make sure. Perhaps he relaxed a bit, knowing he'd be celebrating another victory in less than sixty seconds. Like the rest of the Bruins, he assumed the game was in the bag.

The seconds ticked by. Then, with 49 of them left on the clock and the crowd heading for the exits, the Stars' Kevin Hatcher slammed the puck past Billington. Now the score was 5–4, Boston. Still, time was running out on the Stars. With 16 seconds left, Mike Modano shook loose and lifted the crowd with another Dallas goal. Score tied at five. "Geez," muttered the Bruins in disgust. "Now we'll have to play overtime."

Oh no they didn't. They were in for one more stunning surprise. With a mere five seconds left on the clock, Carbonneau scored again to give the Stars the lead, 6–5. The dazed Bruins gaped in disbelief. They'd blown it. How could they? The game was lost because of three goals in the final minute — three goals in 44.4 seconds to be precise. It was a new team record for the Stars and a humiliating defeat for the Bruins. Billington, along with his shellshocked mates, knew they'd never forget it.

Michael J. Fox and Two Gullible Bruins

T WO former Bruins, Cam Neely and Lyndon Byers, were saddened (as we all were) to hear of Michael J. Fox's struggle with Parkinson's disease. Michael is one of the classiest people in Hollywood and has always had a soft spot in his heart for hockey and for the Boston Bruins. Over the past decade he played in dozens of charity games for the Hollywood All-Stars. When he was filming in Bangkok several years ago, he invited Neely and Byers, who were in Thailand on vacation, to join him on location.

The day before they were to visit, Fox was walking down a Bangkok street when he saw a man with a flute sitting in a pit. The man was a snake charmer. And the pit was full of cobras. Michael watched, fascinated, while the man played his flute and the deadly cobras, swaying gracefully, reacted to the music. As he watched, Michael realized that the cobras posed no real threat to passersby. But tourists were not convinced and recoiled at the sight. Michael moved closer, talked with the snake trainer, gave him some money, and told him he'd be back the next day with some friends.

The following day, after greeting his friends Neely and Byers, Michael J. said, "Guys, let's go for a walk. I've got something neat to show you."

He took them to the snake pit where the piper played and the cobras swayed, their cold, unblinking eyes sizing up the newcomers. Neely and Byers jumped back from the edge of the pit.

"Come on, guys," Michael chided them. "They're just cobras. You two tough hockey players aren't afraid, are you? Well, I'm half your size and I'm not afraid of them. Watch this!"

With that, Michael J. Fox slipped over the edge and into the pit.

"When I did that, Neely and Byers flipped out," Michael laughed, as he related the story. "They screamed and shouted at me, telling me to get the heck out of the pit. Was I crazy or what? They didn't know the snake charmer had told me I'd be perfectly safe if I followed his instructions. And of course I was — and I did. But Neely and Byers thought I was a goner. They thought I was nuts. They almost had simultaneous heart attacks while I was down in that pit. They said it scared the hell out of them.

"And I said, 'Guys, that was the whole idea.'"

Retired Numbers

HISTORICALLY, the Bruins have been one of the quickest NHL teams to retire a star player's number. And, on one occasion, the quickest to unretire one.

For years, in the old Boston Garden, fans could look up to the rafters and see the jerseys of Bruins who had made the franchise memorable. There was Number 2, worn by the incomparable Eddie Shore, the dominant defenseman of his era, from 1926 to 1940.

Over there, Number 3, Lionel Hitchman, Shore's partner along the blueline when the Bruins captured their first Stanley Cup in 1929.

Number 4 appears on Bobby Orr's priceless jersey, representing the best defenseman of all time, the only blueliner to capture an NHL scoring crown.

Number 7 represents Phil Esposito, a scoring machine in the days before Gretzky and Lemieux. The number had been generously given up by Raymond Bourque, who sacrificed it at mid-ice one night, doffing it to hand it to Esposito. Under his Number 7 jersey was another featuring 77, a numeral that's become just as famous now as the single seven.

There is Number 9 for left winger Johnny Bucyk, who came over from the Red Wings after two years' service to play 21 seasons as a Bruin. He became the only 35-year-old to score 51 goals in a season. Bucyk scored 556 goals in his career.

Then a jump to Number 15, worn by much-admired Milt Schmidt, a hardrock Bruin hero from 1936 to 1955.

But wait! We missed Number 5, hanging there in memory of Aubrey "Dit" Clapper, who moved from the town of Newmarket, Ontario, to join the Bruins and stayed for two decades as a right winger and defenseman. He starred on Boston's "Dynamite Line," alongside nimble center Cooney Weiland and left winger Dutch Gainor. Clapper was an integral part of Boston's first three Stanley Cup teams and an All-Star six times. He remains the only All-Star to be named to the team as a forward and a defenseman.

Why, then, would the Bruins hasten to unretire Clapper's number in 1983 and affix it to the back of Guy Lapointe? Lapointe, formerly of Montreal and St. Louis, ended his NHL career in Boston, scoring only two goals in 45 games. The same fans who revered the name Clapper can barely recall Lapointe as a Bruin.

Clapper himself did not want the number unretired. He said as much on his deathbed in 1977. When Harry Sinden approached Clapper's widow, Honey, a few months after her husband's death and suggested that Number 5 be put back into service, she protested, "It's not what Dit would have wanted," she said.

Despite the wishes of the Clapper family, Sinden unretired the number and handed it to Lapointe. Lapointe didn't have the good sense to claim another number for his final season. He and Sinden angered a lot of people by bringing it back, even temporarily.

Hockey writer Leo Monahan, who covered the Bruins for more than 30 years, told *The Hockey News*, "what Sinden's done to Clapper is ghoulish. It's defiling a decent man who entered the Hockey Hall of Fame through the front door, not the side door, like Sinden did."

Nilan Sets a Mark

CHRIS Nilan will never forget the night of March 31, 1991. Playing for the Bruins that night against the Hartford Whalers, Nilan made a record number of trips to the penalty box.

During Boston's 7–3 win over the Whalers in the season finale, Nilan was the game's biggest troublemaker. He accumulated six minors, two majors, one 10-minute misconduct, and one game misconduct — a total of ten penalties. The previous record was nine, held by several players. In a game the previous night, against the Islanders, Nilan had been involved in two fights with Dean Chynoweth. In close, Chynoweth called Nilan "a tired old man." Nilan was so incensed he put the young Islander on his back — twice.

McLaren's the Man

RAY Bourque was winding up his twentieth season as a Boston Bruin, and while he said he "still had lots of hockey to play," reporters couldn't help but wonder who would step in and fill the breach on defense when he retired.

Bourque said he thought Kyle McLaren would be the man. "I see him every day and I'm really impressed with him," Bourque said. "He's really taking charge and he's ready to take over in a lot of ways. I know once I leave, Kyle is going to be the guy the other Bruins look to for leadership. He's ready. Remember, he's only 22 years old and he's got four years of experience behind him. He's got such a bright future in the game."

McLaren, a 6′ 4″ 220-pound defenseman from Humboldt, Saskatchewan, was the Bruins number one draft choice (9th overall) in 1995. He jumped right to the Bruins after two seasons of junior hockey with the Tacoma Rockets.

McLaren doesn't like to think about the day when Ray Bourque won't be around to keep the Bruins on an even keel. And he'd rather not hear talk that he's the logical heir apparent. "Every day I learn something from a great teacher," he says. "I'm not going to be Ray's replacement when he's gone. Nobody can do what he does on the ice. I just try to be the best I can be in every game."

Dafoe Makes Good

THEY say stats don't lie. If that's true, Byron Dafoe is arguably the best goaltender to wear a Bruins' uniform in the past two decades. A check of Dafoe's save percentage in 1998–99, a stat that indicates how well a goaltender performs no matter how badly his team plays in front of him, reveals a superb .926. It's the best by far of any of his recent Bruin predecessors, top stoppers including Andy Moog, Bill Ranford, Reggie Lemelin, and Pete Peeters.

In the past seventeen seasons, only Peeters (.904 in 1982–83) and Blaine Lacher (.902 in 35 games in 1994–95) have compiled save percentages over .900. Dafoe's sparkling .924 record in 1998–99 was compiled despite the fact he faced over 1,800 shots, the most in Bruins' history.

Dafoe's biography is fascinating. He was born in England, where his mother was a staunch admirer of Lord Byron — hence the name. The Dafoe family emigrated to Canada when he was 3, to the town of Comox on Vancouver Island. Not long after settling in, Byron's father left the household, never to return.

His mother remarried and it was his stepfather who introduced him to skating and hockey at age 7. Then his stepfather packed his belongings and left as well.

Even under these unsettling circumstances, young Byron became an excellent all-round athlete. And he was a whiz at school, earning straight A's, and graduating from high school at age 16.

By then he'd become the best goaltending prospect in Comox, and, at age 15, was recruited to play for Victoria, a Tier Two junior club. Most of the players in the league were two, three, even four years older than Dafoe.

After his first season, he was wooed by several U.S. colleges, including Harvard, but he opted to play Junior A hockey with the Portland Winter Hawks. His arch rival in that league was Tri City goaltender Olaf Kolzig, who, like Dafoe, was an immigrant, born in South Africa.

Then, to their dismay, both goaltenders were selected by Washington in the 1989 entry draft. Kolzig was the Caps' first choice, Dafoe the second. Even though they were both returned to junior hockey and served time in the minor pro leagues after that, it meant that some day they'd be battling each other for the number one goaltending job in Washington.

Along the way, they got to know each other, and got to like each other. In the AHL, playing for Portland in 1994, they even shared the Hap Holmes Trophy, awarded to the goaltenders who allowed the fewest goals. In time, they would act as best man at each other's wedding.

Both were called up to play in a handful of games for Washington in 1994–95, but a goaltending surplus there prompted Dafoe to ask for a trade. He was dealt to the L.A. Kings the following July.

Dafoe had been scouted in his minor league days by Gerry Cheevers, who knows a few things about goaltending. Cheevers reported to Boston: "This kid has a bright future. Grab him if you can."

Harry Sinden listened. He made Dafoe one of two prize acquisitions in a 1997 trade with Los Angeles. Dafoe and Dmitri Khristich, the Bruins' goal scoring leader in 1998–99 with 29, came to Boston in return for Jozef Stumpel, Sandy Moger, and a fourth-round draft choice. Dafoe has quickly proved his value and has become a fan favorite at the FleetCenter.

Fascinating Facts About the Bruins

O N December 9, 1941, the Bruins hosted the Blackhawks. But the game was delayed when President Roosevelt told the nation war had been declared against Japan.

The only 16-year-old to play in the NHL was a Boston Bruin. On November 12, 1942, when he was 16 years and 11 months old, Armand "Bep" Guidolin made his NHL debut in a Boston–Toronto game at Maple Leaf Gardens. He was 7–15–22 in 42 games that season and went on to play four years with the Bruins, two with Detroit and four with Chicago.

In the 1929–30 season, the Boston Bruins won all 22 home games and carried their streak to a record 26 wins on home ice through November 18, 1930.

After his hockey career, Jean Pusie became a professional wrestler.

Oldtime trainer Hammy Moore kept busy all season. When he wasn't at the Garden, he ran a golf driving range and a dance hall in Lynnfield, Mass.

On March 4, 1941, the Bruins peppered Chicago goalie Sam LoPresti with 83 shots in a game — an NHL record. Even so, the Bruins won by the narrowest of margins, 3–2.

The Kraut Line (Milt Schmidt, Woody Dumart, and Bobby Bauer) not only played together, lived together, and went off to war together, they negotiated their contracts together with Art Ross. "We took a united front and asked for the same money for the three of us," Schmidt once said. "It worked out well except for 1940 when we asked for a $500 raise because we'd finished 1, 2, 3, in the scoring race. Mr. Ross turned us down."

On October 16, 1949, for the first time, the ice at the Boston Garden was painted. Fans marveled at the difference it made in keeping track of the puck on the white surface.

One night in the mid-sixties, Gordon Drillon, a former Leaf and the last Toronto player to win the NHL scoring title, in 1938, invaded the Boston Garden with a wild band of Maritimers, raised the Canadian flag, and claimed the arena as "a colony of Saint John, New Brunswick. One B's fan commented, "Anybody crazy enough to claim this old barn should be forced to take it."

Bobby Orr's knees gave out after six well-publicized knee operations. But Gord Kluzak, his heir apparent and the first pick overall in 1982, surpassed Bobby's mark with 11 knee surgeries.

In 1970–71 Boston's Phil Esposito set a record for shots on goal with an amazing 550. It broke the previous mark of 414 shots set in 1968–69 by former teammate in Chicago Bobby Hull. Espo's shots paid off in 76 goals, shattering Hull's previous record of 58.

Peter McNab grew up in California where his dad Max ran the San Diego Gulls of the Western Hockey League. Peter was miles behind other players in skills when he went to Denver University. Much hard work made him a prospect and earned him an NHL berth, first with Buffalo, later with the Bruins where he scored 225 of his 363 career goals. He averaged 28 goals per season in eight years as a Bruin.

Chris Hayes, a junior teammate of Bobby Orr, Wayne Cashman, and Nick Beverley, had his name engraved on the 1972 Stanley Cup even though he never played a regular season game for the Bruins — nor did he ever score a point. He played a couple of shifts in one playoff game, entitling him to have his name on the Cup.

The Bruins' Chris Nilan holds the NHL record for most penalties in a game. On March 31, 1991, at the Garden, Nilan was penalized ten times: six minors, two majors, a 10-minute misconduct, and a game misconduct.

In 1982, Harry Sinden and Minnesota North Stars' manager Lou Nanne tried to outsmart each other at the annual draft. Brian

Bellows was the most highly touted junior star and Boston had first choice. But Sinden agreed to pass on Bellows, allowing Nanne, drafting second, to claim him. Why? Because Nanne was willing to give Boston two players, Brad Palmer and Dave Donnelly, in return for the favor. Nanne was delighted to snare Bellows. Sinden said later, "I would have passed on him anyway. I wanted defenseman Gord Kluzak." Hindsight says Sinden should have grabbed Bellows when he had the chance. Bellows, with almost 1,200 NHL games behind him, has collected over 1,000 points and is closing in on 500 goals. Donnelly scored 9 goals in 62 games as a Bruin. Palmer chipped in with 6 goals in 73 games. Numerous knee injuries prevented Kluzak from reaching stardom.

Bobby Lalonde scored a pair of short-handed goals in one period of a playoff game. It happened against Minnesota in 1981.

Boston goalie Pete Peeters embarked on a fabulous undefeated streak in 1982–83. He went 31 games without a loss (26 wins, five ties), one short of Gerry Cheevers' NHL record of 32 games (24 wins and 8 ties).

Gilles Gilbert still holds the NHL record for the longest winning streak by a goaltender — 17 games in 1975–76. Boston netminders Ross Brooks and Tiny Thompson share second place on the list with Don Beaupre (Minnesota) and Tom Barrasso (Pittsburgh) — all with 14 consecutive wins.

Boston goaltender Jim Stewart, called up from the minors on January 10, 1980, because of injuries to the Bruin regulars, allowed five goals on just nine shots in his first period of major league hockey. Stewart and the Bruins lost to St. Louis 7–4. Stewart, a Cambridge native and a college All-American, played another three seasons with no less than ten different pro teams (in five leagues) and never compiled a goals-against average less than 4.00 until he played 7 games with Baltimore in 1981–82 and finished with a 2.59 average.

Eddie Westfall was a key member of the 1970 and 1972 Boston Cup winners but he's best remembered for Stanley Cup heroics elsewhere. In the 1974–75 playoffs, Westfall's New York Islanders won seven straight games on the verge of elimination. In the quarterfinals against Pittsburgh, the Isles rallied from a 3–0 deficit to win the series. In the semifinals versus Philadelphia, the Isles lost the first three games, won the next three, and were defeated 4–1 in the crucial seventh game.

The Bruins helped Mario Lemieux get off to a fast start in the NHL. In his first game, against the Bruins, Lemieux scored on his first shift, on his first shot, against netminder Pete Peeters.

Goalie Byron Dafoe was the best man at Washington goalie Olaf Kolzig's wedding in 1998. Later, Kolzig was best man at Dafoe's wedding. They became good friends when both played for the Capitals.

Only twice in NHL history have players from the same team finished top four in the individual scoring race, and Boston players did it both times. In 1970–71, it was Phil Espositio (152), Bobby Orr (139), Johnny Bucyk (116), and Ken Hodge (105). That season, seven Bruins finished among the top ten scorers. In 1973–74 it was Esposito (145), Orr (122), and Cashman (89).

Burns, Samsonov Take the Spotlight

ON June 25, 1998, Bruins' coach Pat Burns and sensational rookie Sergei Samsonov walked off with major awards at the NHL's annual post-season awards ceremonies in Toronto.

Burns was named the league's top coach and winner of the Jack Adams Award after he presided over the league's biggest turnaround in his first season behind the Boston bench. He guided the youthful Bruins to a 39–30–13 record following a 26–47–9 mark the season before, when they dropped into last place (and out of the playoffs) in the Eastern Conference. They improved by a stunning 30 points. Burns became the first coach in history to capture the award on three occasions — in 1988–89 with the Montreal Canadiens and in 1992–93 with the Toronto

Maple Leafs. Recommended initially for NHL employment by Wayne Gretzky, part-owner of the junior Hull Olympiques when Burns coached there, the former policeman became the second Bruin to win the Adams Award since its inception in 1973–74. The first was Don Cherry in 1975–76.

Sergei Samsonov joined an impressive list of Bruins whose names are on the Calder Trophy. He is listed along with goalies Frank Brimsek (1939) and Jack Gelineau (1950), forwards Larry Regan (1957) and Derek Sanderson (1968), and defensemen Bobby Orr (1967) and Ray Bourque (1980). Samsonov led all first-year players in 1997–98 with 22 goals and 25 assists for 47 points in a season when all rookies struggled to match the totals of previous Calder Trophy winners such as Teemu Selanne (76 goals, 132 points) and Mario Lemieux (43 goals, 100 points). Regan's stats in 1957 were 14–19–33, and Sanderson's were 25–24–49. In his sophomore season, Samsonov scored 25–26–51.

A native of Moscow, Samsonov has been destined for stardom since he played a series of exhibition games in Canada in June 1994. On tour, the stocky 15-year-old appeared to be the second coming of Pavel Bure and Wayne Gretzky combined. Sergei Gimaev, his coach at that time, said, "He's better than Bure was at this age." Other coaches of the teams he faced mentioned Gretzky when they were asked to assess young Samsonov's incredible skating ability and puck handling skills.

The Calder wasn't Samsonov's first rookie award. A year earlier, after scoring 29 goals with the Detroit Vipers in the International Hockey League, he was named that circuit's best freshman player.

Thornton Coming On

A month before his eighteenth birthday Joe Thornton became only the second 17-year-old to be drafted number one overall (Pierre Turgeon was the other) and he was thrilled to think he'd soon become a member of the Boston Bruins.

Bobby Orr predicted a bright future for Thornton. "He's going to be a great player in the NHL for a long time. He'll handle the pressure. One look at that big smile on his face and you know he just loves playing the game."

Assistant general manager Mike O'Connell said, "We know the Bruins have a special player. He'll be frustrated at first by the speed and size of other players. The big thing will be building up his confidence. There are not too many players — Eric Lindros is one and Joe is another — who would be the first choice of all the teams drafting from the amateur ranks."

Thornton signed a three-year contract with the Bruins under which he could earn, with bonuses, almost $3 million (U.S.) annually. In his rookie season, he earned his $925,000 base salary and could have cashed some huge bonuses if he'd scored 60 points. Of course, that was expecting far too much from one so young. Even the best of the Junior stars find it a giant leap to the pace and physical grind of the NHL.

Thornton scored only 3 goals in his first season (in 55 games) and added 4 assists. Many of his fans were disappointed. They were hoping he'd come close to duplicating his final year junior stats when he scored 41 goals and 122 points with Sault Ste. Marie.

In his first 27 games as a sophomore, he scored only twice. Then, in the next 27 games, he collected 9 goals and finished his sophomore season with 16 goals and 25 assists for 41 points.

Coach Pat Burns is pleased with his young star's progress. "He's looking more comfortable all the time," Burns remarked. "He turned 20 on July 2 and he's a man now. He's been around the league a couple of times. He's ready to blossom."

Anyone still concerned about Thornton's future should review the assessment of Thornton made by Central Scouting in his draft year. It reads: "An excellent skater with a powerful stride, explosive speed and strong balance . . . able to deceive opponents through rapid changes of pace . . . has exceptional puckhandling skills . . . has a unique vision of the ice and is able to create and find the open spaces . . . is a powerful shooter and an accurate passer . . . is an opportunist around the net . . . is a finesse player who possesses a tremendous amount of aggression . . . will face up to any challenge and has the ability to dominate a game . . . is mentally tough and holds an excellent attitude toward the game . . . is an unselfish player with a strong work ethic . . . a team leader."

With that kind of endorsement, how can he miss?

Bruins Rewarded
for Excellence

FROM Eddie Shore's four Hart Trophies in seven years, Phil Esposito's five Art Ross Trophies as the NHL's leading scorer, to Bobby Orr's and Ray Bourque's incredible domination of the Norris Trophy (13 in all), the Boston Bruins' list of players who've been rewarded for excellence is a long and impressive one. Here are the Bruins who've won league honors over the years.

Lady Byng Memorial Trophy
(sportsmanship and gentlemanly conduct)

Bobby Bauer — 1940, 1941, 1947
Don McKenney — 1960
John Bucyk — 1971, 1974
Jean Ratelle — 1976
Rick Middleton — 1982

— **Herb Cain** was runner-up to Clint Smith in 1944
— **Woody Dumart** was runner-up to Red Kelly in 1951
— **John Bucyk** was runner-up to Stan Mikita in 1968,
    Phil Goyette in 1970, Ratelle in 1972, and Marcel Dionne
    in 1975
— **Jean Ratelle** was runner-up to Marcel Dionne in 1977
— **Peter McNab** was runner-up to Butch Goring in 1978
— **Rick Middleton** was runner-up to Mike Bossy in 1983
    and 1984
— **Adam Oates** was runner-up to Pierre Turgeon in 1993,
    Wayne Gretzky in 1994, Ron Francis in 1995, and Paul
    Kariya in 1996

James Norris Memorial Trophy
(best defenseman)

> Bobby Orr — 1968, 1969, 1970, 1971, 1972, 1973,
>   1974, 1975
> Ray Bourque — 1987, 1988, 1990, 1991, 1994

— Brad Park was runner-up to Denis Potvin in 1976 and 1978
— Ray Bourque was runner-up to Doug Wilson in 1982,
   Paul Coffey in 1985, Brian Leetch in 1992, and Chris
   Chelios in 1993 and 1996

Hart Memorial Trophy
(most valuable player to his team)

> Eddie Shore — 1933, 1935, 1936, 1938
> Bill Cowley — 1941, 1943
> Milt Schmidt — 1951
> Phil Esposito — 1969, 1974
> Bobby Orr — 1970, 1971, 1972

— Sprague Cleghorn was runner-up to Nels Stewart in 1926
— Lionel Hitchman was runner-up to Nels Stewart in 1930
— Eddie Shore was runner-up to Howie Morenz in 1931
— Dit Clapper was runner-up to Bill Cowley in 1941
— Bill Cowley was runner-up to Babe Pratt in 1944
— Milt Schmidt was runner-up to Maurice Richard in 1947
— Frank Brimsek was runner-up to Buddy O'Connor in 1948
— Phil Esposito was runner-up to Bobby Orr in 1971 and
   Bobby Clarke in 1973
— Pete Peeters was runner-up to Wayne Gretzky in 1983
— Ray Bourque was runner-up to Wayne Gretzky in 1987
   and Mark Messier in 1990

Vezina Trophy
(best goaltender)

> Cecil "Tiny" Thompson — 1930, 1933, 1936, 1938
> Frank Brimsek — 1939, 1942
> Pete Peeters — 1983

— Tiny Thompson was runner-up to George Hainsworth
  in 1929
— Frank Brimsek was runner-up to Dave Kerr in 1940, Turk
  Broda in 1941 (with Johnny Mowers), and Bill Durnan
  in 1946
— Gilles Gilbert was runner-up to Bernie Parent and Tony
  Esposito in 1974
— Gilles Gilbert and Gerry Cheevers were runners-up to
  Bob Sauve and Don Edwards in 1980

Art Ross Trophy
(leading point scorer)

> Ralph "Cooney" Weiland — 1930
> Milt Schmidt — 1940
> Bill Cowley — 1941
> Herb Cain — 1944
> Phil Esposito — 1969, 1971, 1972, 1973, 1974
> Bobby Orr — 1970, 1975

— Woody Dumart was runner-up to Milt Schmidt in 1940
— Bill Cowley was runner-up to Doug Bentley in 1943
— Bronco Hovath was runner-up to Bobby Hull in 1960
— Phil Esposito was runner-up to Stan Mikita in 1968 and
  Bobby Orr in 1970 and 1975
— Bobby Orr was runner-up to Phil Esposito in 1971, 1972,
  and 1974

Calder Memorial Trophy
(top rookie)

    Frank Brimsek — 1939
    Jack Gelineau — 1950
    Larry Regan — 1957
    Bobby Orr — 1967
    Derek Sanderson — 1968
    Ray Bourque — 1980
    Sergei Samsonov — 1998

— Roy Conacher was runner-up to Frank Brimsek in 1939
— Ken Smith was runner-up to Frank McCool in 1945
— Pete Babando was runner-up to Jim McFadden in 1948
— Phil Maloney was runner-up to Jack Gelineau in 1950
— Don McKenney was runner-up to Ed Litzenberger in 1955
— Cliff Pennington was runner-up to Bobby Rousseau in 1962
— Barry Pederson was runner-up to Dale Hawerchuk in 1982
— Joe Juneau was runner-up to Teemu Selanne in 1993

Frank J. Selke Trophy
(best defensive forward)

    Steve Kasper — 1982

— Don Marcotte was runner-up to Bob Gainey in 1979
— Steve Kasper was runner-up to Guy Carbonneau in 1988
— Dave Poulin was runner-up to Doug Gilmour in 1993

Conn Smythe Trophy
(playoff MVP)

    Bobby Orr — 1970, 1972

Lester Patrick Trophy
(for outstanding service to hockey in the U.S.)

Charles Adams — 1967
Walter Brown — 1968
Eddie Shore — 1970
Ralph "Cooney" Weiland — 1972
Weston Adams, Sr. — 1974
John Bucyk — 1977
Phil Esposito — 1978
Tom Fitzgerald — 1978
Bobby Orr — 1979
Art Ross — 1984
Fred Cusick — 1988
Joe Mullen — 1995
Milt Schmidt — 1996
Harry Sinden — 1999

Bill Masterson Trophy
(for perserverence, sportsmanship, and dedication to hockey)

Charlie Simmer — 1986
Gord Kluzak — 1990
Cam Neely — 1994

Lester B. Pearson Award
(outstanding performer selected by the NHLPA)

Phil Esposito — 1971, 1974
Bobby Orr — 1975

William M. Jennings Trophy
(goaltender(s) with fewest goals against)

Andy Moog and Reggie Lemelin — 1990

— Pete Peeters was runner-up to Roland Melanson
and Billy Smith in 1983

King Clancy Memorial Trophy
(leadership and humanitarian contributions to his community)

    Ray Bourque — 1992
    Dave Poulin — 1993

Jack Adams Award
(coach of the year)

    Don Cherry — 1976
    Pat Burns — 1998

— **Don Cherry** was runner-up to Bobby Kromm in 1978
— **Mike Milbury** was runner-up to Bob Murdoch in 1990
— **Brian Sutter** was runner-up to Pat Burns in 1993

THE BRUINS
THROUGH THE YEARS

1924–25 THE BOSTON BRUINS ARE GRANTED an NHL franchise for a fee of $15,000. Art Ross named manager of first NHL team in U.S. On December 1, 1924, the first NHL game ever played in the U.S. features the Bruins and the Maroons at the Boston Arena. The Bruins win 2–1. They finish in last place in the six-team league.

1925–26 THE BRUINS PURCHASE LIONEL HITCHMAN from Ottawa. Despite a 17–3–1 streak to end the season, the Bruins finish in fourth place. Jimmy Herberts leads the team in scoring with 31 points.

1926–27 EDDIE SHORE MAKES HIS NHL DEBUT in the season opener against the Canadiens. In their third season, the Bruins reach the Stanley Cup finals, and lose to the Ottawa Senators.

1927–28 DIT CLAPPER SCORES HIS FIRST NHL GOAL in the November 15 season opener — a 1–1 tie against Chicago. Goaltender Hal Winkler starts in all 44 games, finishing with 15 shutouts and a 1.59 goals-against average. The Bruins finish first in the American Division but are knocked out of the playoffs in the first round by the Rangers.

1928–29 THE BRUINS SUFFER A 1–0 LOSS to the Canadiens in their first game at the new Boston Garden. On January 3, 1929, Eddie Shore misses the train to Montreal, drives all night through a blizzard, then scores the only goal of the game in a 1–0 Boston victory over the Maroons. The "Dynamite Line" of Weiland, Clapper, and Gainor lead the Bruins to first place in the American Division. The B's bring home their first Stanley Cup on March 29, when they beat the Rangers 2–1 in Game Two of the best-of-three final series.

1929–30 THE BRUINS WIN 38 OF 44 GAMES played, win all 22 of their home games, and finish with the best record in the league. They enjoy a 14-game win streak from December to January 12. Cooney Weiland leads the league in scoring with 43 goals. The Dynamite Line scores 102 of the team's 179 goals. Despite a stellar season, the Bruins lose the Stanley Cup to Montreal, 2–0.

1930–31 THE BRUINS CONTINUE TO DOMINATE the American Division of the NHL. On March 18, 1930, Cooney Weiland collects a hat trick in a 9–2 win over the Rangers in the final game of the season, giving him a league-record 73 points (in 44 games). The Bruins are ousted from the playoffs in the semifinal round by Montreal, three games to two. On March 26, Art Ross becomes the first NHL coach to pull his goalie and send out an extra attacker.

1931–32 DUTCH GAINOR, A MEMBER OF THE DYNAMITE LINE, is traded for Joe Jerwa, a player who doesn't play a single game all season in a Bruin uniform. The season is filled with disappointments as the Bruins finish last in the league and out of the playoffs.

1932–33 THE BRUINS REBOUND THANKS to Eddie Shore and Tiny Thompson. Shore wins the Hart Trophy and Thompson the Vezina. George Owen becomes the first U.S.–born player to score a hat trick. The Bruins and the Leafs play the longest overtime (to that time) in NHL history: 104 minutes and 46 seconds, with the Leafs winning on Doraty's goal. The Bruins top the American Division standings, but lose to Toronto in the first round of the playoffs.

1933–34 IN A DECEMBER 12 GAME AT THE BOSTON GARDEN, Eddie Shore deals a vicious check on Toronto's Ace Bailey, who suffers a fractured skull and almost dies. Shore is suspended for 16 games. Lionel Hitchman retires. The Bruins finish in last place in their division.

1934–35 ART ROSS ASSUMES FULL-TIME GENERAL managing duties while Frank Patrick takes over as coach of the Bruins. The club soars to first place in the American Division. Eddie Shore wins the Hart Trophy. The Bruins bow out in the playoffs in the opening round.

1935–36 TINY THOMPSON PLAYS IN ALL 48 GAMES, notching 10 shutouts and earning a goals-against average of 1.73. On March 17 he becomes the first goaltender to earn an assist in a game. The Bruins collect 50 points to finish in second place behind Detroit. They exit from the playoffs with a first-round loss to Toronto.

1936–37 ART ROSS RETURNS TO THE BENCH as Bruins coach. The team loses Eddie Shore for the season after he suffers a cracked vertebra. The Bruins compile a record of 23–18–7 for a second-place finish behind Detroit. Tiny Thompson stops the Maroons' Lionel Conacher on the first-ever playoff penalty shot. The Maroons eliminate the Bruins in the first round, three games to one.

1937–38 THE "KRAUT LINE" OF MILT SCHMIDT, Bobby Bauer, and Woody Dumart makes its debut, accounting for 46 Boston goals, despite the loss of Schmidt for a month with a broken jaw. Tiny Thompson wins the Vezina and Shore skates off with another Hart Trophy. The Bruins finish first in the American Division but bow out of the playoffs with an opening-round loss to Toronto.

1938–39 THE NHL SWITCHES TO A SINGLE DIVISION. The Bruins finish on top with a record of 36–10–2. Tiny Thompson is sold to Detroit and rookie Frank Brimsek, with six shutouts in his first eight games, proves to be an outstanding replacement. His 10 shutouts and 1.58 goals-against average earn him the Calder and Vezina trophies. The Bruins establish a record by going 37 games undefeated in overtime. Mel "Sudden Death" Hill scores three overtime goals in the playoffs and the Bruins capture their second Stanley Cup by defeating Toronto 4–1.

1939–40 VETERAN EDDIE SHORE IS TRADED TO the New York Americans for Eddie Wiseman. The Bruins have the top three scorers in the NHL in Milt Schmidt, Woody Dumart, and Lady Byng winner Bobby Bauer. Bill Cowley finishes fifth. Cooney Weiland takes over as coach. The Bruins finish atop the league standings but are ousted in the first round of the playoffs by the Rangers, four games to two.

1940–41 THE BRUINS DOMINATE AGAIN and finish with a 27–8–13 record. In the months of January, February, and March, the B's lose only one game. They compile a 23-game unbeaten streak from December 21 to February 25 and take a record 83 shots at Chicago netminder Sam LoPresti on March 4. Bobby Bauer wins the Lady Byng and Bill Cowley, who leads the NHL in scoring, takes home the Hart Trophy. The Bruins sweep Detroit in the finals to win their third Stanley Cup.

1941–42 THE BRUINS LOSE NUMEROUS PLAYERS TO military duty, including all three members of the Kraut Line. Art Ross resigns as governor of the Bruins and is replaced by R.R. Duncan. The Bruins finish third in the league and are knocked out of the playoffs in the second round by Detroit.

1942–43 THE "SPROUT LINE" OF BILL SHILL, Don Gallinger, and Bep Guidolin tries to replace the Kraut Line. At 16, Guidolin is the youngest player in NHL history. The Bruins finish four points back of Detroit and are swept by the Red Wings in the Stanley Cup finals.

1943–44 HERB CAIN AMASSES 82 POINTS to break the record formerly held by Cooney Weiland. Frank Brimsek joins the Coast Guard and is replaced by Bert Gardiner. When Gardiner is pulled late in a November 11 game, the Rangers' Clint Smith scores the first empty-net goal in NHL history. The Bruins finish in fifth place and miss the playoffs for the first time in ten years.

1944–45 THE BRUINS SCORE A TEAM-RECORD 14 GOALS in a game against New York. The B's set a league record for fastest four goals in the 14–3 rout, scoring them in a span of 1:20. The B's finish in fourth place, a whopping 44 points behind first-place Montreal. They lose to Detroit in seven games in the first playoff round.

1945–46 ART ROSS RETIRES FROM COACHING and is succeeded by Dit Clapper, who becomes the first playing coach in Bruins history. Brimsek, Schmidt, Bauer, and Dumart all return from the war. The Bruins finish five points behind league-leading Montreal. In the finals they lose to Montreal in five games.

1946–47 BOSTON GAMES ARE BROADCAST ON RADIO (over WHDH) with Frank Ryan and Leo Egan as commentators. Dit Clapper hangs up his skates, his Number 5 is retired and he is immediately inducted into the Hockey Hall of Fame. Eddie Shore's Number 2 also is retired. The Kraut Line leads the team in scoring. Bauer wins his third Lady Byng Trophy. The

Bruins finish in third place but are eliminated in the semifinals by the Canadiens in five games.

1947–48 FRANK BRIMSEK PLAYS ALL 60 GAMES for the Bruins. Bobby Bauer retires. The Bruins finish with a losing record at 23–24–13 but still place third in the league standings. The B's lose to the eventual Cup-winners, the Toronto Maple Leafs, in the first round of the playoffs. Boston's Don Gallinger suspended for life for associating with gamblers and wagering on games.

1948–49 THE SPOKED "B" MAKES ITS FIRST appearance on the Bruins' jerseys in celebrations of the team's 25th anniversary. John Peirson finishes as the club's leading scorer with 43 points. Frank Brimsek takes a six-game leave of absence to be with his critically ill son, who later dies. The Bruins finish in second place but lose to Toronto for the second year in a row in the first round of the playoffs. The Art Ross Trophy is now awarded annually to the scoring leader, not the MVP, and Montreal's Elmer Lach is the first winner.

1949–50 ROOKIE JACK GELINEAU TAKES OVER in goal for Boston and wins the Calder Trophy. Center Phil Maloney is second in the balloting. The B's trade for Bill Quackenbush and Pete Horeck. They win just three of their final 13 games and finish in fifth place, out of the playoffs for the first time in six years.

1950–51 LYNN PATRICK COACHES HIS FIRST OF FIVE seasons, replacing George Boucher. Milt Schmidt leads the team in scoring with 61 points and wins the Hart Trophy. The Bruins finish eight games under .500 but still capture fourth place. They face Toronto in the first round of the playoffs and lose in six games.

___

1951–52 WESTON ADAMS RESIGNS HIS POSITION as president of the Bruins. Walter Brown, the general manager of the Boston Garden, succeeds him and purchases 60 percent of the team. A game in February is transferred to the Boston Arena because of collapsed brine pipes in the Garden. Only 4,049 fans show up. The Bruins finish in fourth place and are eliminated in seven games by Montreal in the first playoff round.

1952–53 THE FIRST NHL GAME IS TELEVISED on the Canadian Broadcasting Corporation on November 1. It features the Bruins and the Leafs. Fred Cusick makes his announcing debut on WHDH radio. Sugar Jim Henry plays all 70 games in goal for the Bruins. Fleming Mackell leads the team in scoring with 44 points. The Bruins finish in third place and knock the Red Wings out in the first round of the playoffs before losing to Montreal in the finals.

1953–54 THE BRUINS LEAD THE LEAGUE in penalty minutes with 685. Art Ross retires as general manager and is replaced by Lynn Patrick. The B's post three consecutive shutouts on Boston Garden ice. On November 14, both Bill Quakenbush and Real Chevrefils suffer broken legs. The Bruins finish in fourth place and are swept aside by Montreal in the opening round of the playoffs.

1954–55 WOODY DUMART AND MILT SCHMIDT RETIRE. Sugar Jim Henry and Long John Henderson share the goaltending duties. Leo Labine and Don McKenney tie for the team lead in scoring with 42 points. The Bruins finish in fourth place and are eliminated in the first playoff round by the Canadiens.

$1955\text{--}56$ JOHN PEIRSON IS COAXED OUT OF RETIRE-
MENT and returns to the Bruins. Milt Schmidt coaches full time.
In a November 5 game, Jean Beliveau scores 4 goals against the
B's, including three in 44 seconds during a power play. This feat
prompts NHL to change a rule: minor penalties will now end
after a power-play goal is scored. The Bruins are shut out 11 times,
more than any other club. They score the fewest goals in the
league — 147. They finish in fifth place and miss the playoffs.

$1956\text{--}57$ HAL LAYCOE AND BILL QUACKENBUSH
RETIRE. Terry Sawchuk plays 34 games in goal but is hospitalized
with mononucleosis in December and eventually is traded back
to Detroit. The B's acquire Johnny Bucyk in the deal. CBS tele-
vises an NHL game for the first time. The Bruins finish in third
place and advance to the Stanley Cup finals where they lose in
five games to Montreal.

$1957\text{--}58$ WILLIE O'REE, THE FIRST BLACK PLAYER
in the NHL, skates on a line with Jerry Toppazzini and Don
McKenney. Toppazzini scores seven shorthanded goals during
the season. Johnny Bucyk scores a hat trick in his debut as a
Bruin. The B's earn fourth place and defeat the Rangers in six
games in the opening playoff round. In the finals, the B's lose to
Montreal in six.

$1958\text{--}59$ FIVE BRUINS SCORE HAT TRICKS DURING
the season. On February 8, Bronco Horvath scores a hat trick that
includes two shorthanded goals. The Bruins have the fewest
major penalties of any team. They finish in second place with a
32–29–9 mark but lose to Toronto in seven games in the opening
playoff round.

1959–60 BRONCO HORVATH ENJOYS A 22-GAME point-scoring streak. He loses the scoring title to Bobby Hull by one point. Goalie Don Simmons becomes the first Boston goaltender, and the second after Jacques Plante, to wear a face mask. Don McKenney wins the Lady Byng Trophy. The Bruins miss the playoffs by three points.

1960–61 JERRY TOPPAZZINI BECOMES THE LAST non-goalie to take over for an injured netminder when he replaces Don Simmons for a few minutes in a 5–2 loss to Chicago. The Bruins manage just two road wins while suffering 25 losses. They allow the most goals (254) and finish with the most losses (42). They finish out of the playoffs for the second straight year. Phil Watson is named new coach in June, replacing Milt Schmidt.

1961–62 THE BRUINS OPEN THE SEASON WITH an eight-game losing streak. They endure a 20-game losing streak later in the season. They sign 14-year-old Bobby Orr to a player development contract. Leo Labine and Vic Stasiuk are dealt to Detroit. The B's finish with just 15 wins and settle in last place, missing the playoffs for the third straight year.

1962–63 THE BRUINS SHUT OUT MONTREAL 5–0 in the opener but win only 13 more games all season. They surrender a league-high 281 goals and suffer through a 10-game winless streak. Tommy Williams sets a record for a U.S.–born player with his 21st goal. The B's finish in last place and do not qualify for the playoffs. They draft goalie Ed Johnston from the Montreal organization.

1963–64 ON DECEMBER 4, ANDY HEBENTON PLAYS in his 581st consecutive game, breaking Johnny Wilson's iron-man record. Ed Johnston becomes the last goalie to play in every minute of all of his team's games. Murray Oliver leads the team with 68 points. The Bruins finish last, out of the playoffs.

1964–65 THE BRUINS OPEN WITH A NINE-GAME winless streak. Johnny Bucyk leads the team in scoring with 55 points. The B's are shut out six times. They select goalie Ken Dryden in the amateur draft but trade away his rights to Montreal for Guy Allen and Paul Reid. The Bruins win 21 games, their best record in five years, but still finish in last place.

1965–66 DRAFTED FROM TORONTO, GERRY CHEEVERS makes his Bruin debut. So does rookie Bernie Parent. The Bruins trade Reg Fleming to New York for John McKenzie. Murray Oliver leads the team in points with 60. The Bruins finish with the same 21–43–6 record as the season before but manage to escape the NHL basement, finishing one point ahead of the Rangers.

1966–67 BOBBY ORR ARRIVES! He earns the Calder Trophy as rookie of the year. Harry Sinden replaces Milt Schmidt behind the bench. Gerry Cheevers, Bernie Parent and Ed Johnston share the goaltending duties. Johnny Bucyk sets a club record with his 576th career point. The Bruins return to the league basement with a 17–43–10 record.

1967–68 THE NHL EXPANDS TO TWELVE TEAMS. Derek Sanderson scores 24 goals and wins the Calder Trophy. Bobby Orr wins the Norris. The Bruins swing a blockbuster deal with Chicago and acquire Phil Esposito, Ken Hodge, and Fred Stanfield for Gilles Marotte, Pit Martin, and goalie Jack Norris.

The Bruins finish in third place in the new Eastern Division and reach the playoffs for the first time in eight years. They lose four straight to Montreal in the first round.

1968–69 PHIL ESPOSITO BECOMES THE FIRST PLAYER to score 100 points in a season, finishing with 126. He wins the Art Ross and Hart trophies. Bobby Orr sets a record for goals (21) and points (64) by a defenseman and captures the Norris Trophy. The Bruins enjoy an 18-game undefeated streak and finish in second place in the Eastern Division. They sweep the Leafs in the first playoff round but lose to Montreal in the semifinals.

1969–70 THE BRUINS ENJOY A 17-GAME undefeated streak on Garden ice. They tie Chicago for most points in the NHL with 99. They defeat the Rangers in six games in the first round of the playoffs, then sweep the next two series to win their first Stanley Cup in 29 years. Bobby Orr collects the Conn Smythe Trophy as playoff MVP, as well as the Hart, the Ross (a first for a defenseman), and the Norris. Harry Sinden resigns to enter the business world.

1970–71 THE BRUINS, WITH 57 WINS, set 37 individual and team records. They enjoy a 13-game winning streak on their way to first place with 121 points. Bobby Orr earns his second straight Hart Trophy and his fourth Norris. Johnny Bucyk becomes the oldest player to score more than 50 goals in a season. Bucyk is awarded the Lady Byng and Phil Esposito takes home the Art Ross Trophy as leading scorer. The Bruins are upset in the first round of the playoffs by Montreal.

1971–72 THE BRUINS FINISH ATOP THE LEAGUE for the second year in a row, this time with a 54–13–11 record, good for 119 points. Phil Esposito scores 133 points to win his second consecutive Art Ross Trophy. The Bruins defeat Toronto and

St. Louis on their way to the Stanley Cup finals. Bobby Orr scores the Cup-winning goal for the second time in his career when the Bruins beat the Rangers in six games. Orr wins his second Conn Smythe Trophy, his third consecutive Hart, and his fifth consecutive Norris.

1972–73 HARRY SINDEN RETURNS AS GENERAL MANAGER. For the third year in a row, Phil Esposito captures the Ross Trophy as the NHL's leading scorer (130 points). Bobby Orr, with 101 points, wins his sixth straight Norris Trophy. The Bruins enjoy a 10-game winning streak and finish in second place in the Eastern Division. They suffer a first-round playoff loss to the New York Rangers.

1973–74 GOALIE ROSS BROOKS, a 36-year-old rookie, records 14 consecutive victories on his way to a 16–3–0 record. Bobby Orr has a seven-point night against the Rangers and is named the Norris Trophy winner for the seventh year in a row. Phil Esposito compiles 145 points to win the Art Ross Trophy for the fourth consecutive season. He also wins the Hart Trophy. The Bruins finish with 113 points, a league high. They sweep Toronto and eliminate Chicago in six games before losing to Philadelphia in the finals in six games. Don Cherry replaces Bep Guidolin as the Bruins coach.

1974–75 DEREK SANDERSON IS TRADED to the Rangers for Walt McKechnie. Bobby Orr wins the Art Ross Trophy for his 135-point season and captures his eighth consecutive Norris Trophy. The Bruins finish in second place in the new Adams Division. They lose in the three-game preliminary round of the playoffs to the Chicago Blackhawks.

1975–76 JOHNNY BUCYK SCORES HIS 500TH career goal. Bobby Orr undergoes two knee operations and plays in just 10 games. The Bruins enjoy a 20-game home undefeated streak. The Bruins obtain Brad Park, Jean Ratelle, and Joe Zanussi from the Rangers in return for Phil Esposito and Carol Vadnais. With 113 points, the Bruins finish in first place in the Adams. They defeat the Los Angeles Kings in seven games but are eliminated by Philadelphia, the defending Stanley Cup champs, in the semi-finals. Don Cherry is named coach of the year.

1976–77 THE BRUINS TRADE KEN HODGE to the Rangers in return for Rick Middleton. In his first full season as a Bruin, Jean Ratelle leads the team in scoring with 94 points. Johnny Bucyk is named co-winner of the Lester Patrick Award for outstanding service to hockey in the U.S. The Bruins finish in first place in the Adams Division. They eliminate the Kings in the first playoff round and sweep Philadelphia in the second round. They are swept by Montreal in the finals.

1977–78 TERRY O'REILLY BECOMES THE FIRST player in NHL history to finish in the top ten in scoring while racking 200 or more penalty minutes. He leads the Bruins in points with 90. The Bruins enjoy an 11-game home winning streak and finish first in the Adams Division. They boast eleven 20-goal scorers, an NHL record. They sweep Chicago in the first round and defeat the flyers in five games in the second round. They lose to Montreal in the Stanley Cup finals.

1978–79 RICK MIDDLETON LEADS THE BRUINS in scoring with 86 points. Bobby Orr's Number 4 jersey is retired before a January 9 exhibition game against the Soviet Wings. The Bruins sweep Pittsburgh in the first playoff round. In Game Seven of the semifinal series against Montreal, Cherry's team is caught with too many men on the ice and they lose the series. Sinden fires Cherry and hires Fred Creighton as coach.

1979–80 THE BRUINS SELECT RAY BOURQUE with their first pick of the amateur draft. Bourque sets an NHL record for rookie defensemen with 65 points. Terry O'Reilly breaks his own team mark for penalty minutes with 265. The Bruins retire Johnny Bucyk's Number 9 on March 13. The Bruins settle for second place in the Adams Division and defeat Pittsburgh in the first playoff round. They lose to the eventual Stanley Cup champions, the New York Islanders, in round two.

1980–81 GERRY CHEEVERS TAKES OVER AS COACH. Keith Crowder sets a team record for penalty minutes in a game with 43. Goaltender Jim Craig, an Olympic hero, is acquired from Calgary and enjoys a seven-game unbeaten streak. Rick Middleton leads the Bruins in scoring with 103 points. The Bruins finish in second place in the Adams Division and are ousted from the playoffs in the first round by the Minnesota North Stars.

1981–82 RICK MIDDLETON, WITH 51 GOALS, BECOMES the first Bruin to top 50 goals since Phil Esposito in 1975. Barry Pederson breaks the rookie goal-scoring mark with 44. His 92 points put him second to Middleton among Bruin scorers. Keith and Bruce Crowder are the first brothers to play for Boston since Max and Bill Quackenbush in 1950–51. The Bruins eliminate Buffalo in the first round of the playoffs but are ousted by Quebec in round two. In the entry draft, the Bruins use the first pick overall to draft Gord Kluzak.

1982–83 BRAD MCCRIMMON IS TRADED TO Philadelphia for goaltender Pete Peeters who enjoys a 31-game undefeated streak with 26 wins and 5 ties. On October 23 in Vancouver, the Bruins' Normand Leveille suffers a cerebral hemorrhage and his promising career is ended. The Bruins finish with the best overall record in the league, 50–20–10. They eliminate

Quebec and Buffalo in the first two rounds of the playoffs, only to fall to the New York Islanders in the Wales Conference finals.

1983–84 THE NHL REINSTATES OVERTIME and Rick Middleton becomes the first Bruin to score in overtime in more than 40 years. Ray Bourque becomes only the sixth defenseman in history to score 30 goals. The Bruins finish tied with the Islanders for the second-best record overall, 104 points. But they manage only two goals in the first round of the playoffs and are eliminated by Montreal.

1984–85 THE BRUINS SCORE MORE THAN 300 GOALS for the fifteenth consecutive season. They finish the season just above .500 with a 36–34–10 mark for fourth place in the Adams Division. They make a quick exit from the playoffs after a first-round loss to the Canadiens.

1985–86 AFTER TALLYING HIS 400TH CAREER GOAL, Rick Middleton's season comes to a halt because of a concussion. Assistant coach Mike Milbury steps off the bench to help out on defense for 22 games. The Bruins finish in third place in the Adams Division and are eliminated in the first round of the play-offs for the third consecutive year. In June, the Bruins obtain Cam Neely (and a draft choice who turns out to be Glen Wesley) from Vancouver for Barry Pederson.

1986–87 IN HIS FIRST SEASON AS A BRUIN, CAM NEELY finishes second to Ray Bourque in team scoring. Bourque wins the Norris Trophy as the NHL's top defenseman. Coach Butch Goring is fired and Terry O'Reilly takes his place. Knee problems keep Gord Kluzak out of the lineup for the season. The Bruins finish in third place in the Adams Division and are swept aside by the Canadiens in the first round of the playoffs.

1987–88 BOSTON'S KEN LINSEMAN AND THE BLUES' DOUG GILMOUR score goals two seconds apart in a December 19 game. Jay Miller breaks the team record for penalty minutes with 302. On December 3, Phil Esposito Night, Ray Bourque changes his Number 7 to Number 77. The Bruins finish second in the Wales Conference. They defeat Buffalo in the first round of the playoffs, then eliminate Montreal for the first time in 45 years. After ousting New Jersey, they reach the Cup finals for the first time in six years. A power failure at the Garden forces postponement of Game Four. The Bruins fail to win a game in the finals.

1988–89 CAM NEELY ENJOYS HIS THIRD STRAIGHT SEASON of more than 30 goals. For the 22nd season in a row the Bruins compile a winning record and qualify for the playoffs. Their 37–29–14 record places them second to Montreal in the Adams Division. The Bruins beat the Sabres in the first round but are eliminated by Montreal in the division finals.

1989–90 REGGIE LEMELIN AND ANDY MOOG WIN the Jennings Trophy for allowing the fewest goals in the league, 232. Moog sets a playoff record for the B's by playing 1,196 minutes. The Bruins compile a 46–25–9 record for top spot in the league. Dave Poulin is acquired from Philadelphia for Ken Linseman. Ray Bourque wins the Norris Trophy and Gord Kluzak, who plays in only 8 games, is awarded the Bill Masterton Trophy. The Bruins defeat Hartford, Montreal, and Washington en route to the Stanley Cup finals, where they lose in five games to the Edmonton Oilers.

1990–91 RAY BOURQUE PLAYS IN HIS 800TH GAME and leads the Bruins in scoring for the fourth time in his career. He wins the Norris Trophy for the second year in a row. Cam Neely enjoys an eight-game goal scoring streak. Chris Nilan sets a league record with 10 penalties in one game. The Bruins lead the Wales Conference with 100 points. They defeat Hartford in six games and the Canadiens in seven before being eliminated by Pittsburgh, the eventual Stanley Cup winners.

1991–92 RICK BOWNESS TAKES OVER AS COACH, replacing Mike Milbury. Craig Janney and Stephane Quintal are sent to the Blues in return for Adam Oates. The Bruins require seven games to oust Buffalo in the first round for the playoffs but need only four to eliminate Montreal — their first sweep of the Habs in more than 60 years. The Bruins are swept in four games by Pittsburgh.

1992–93 BRIAN SUTTER BECOMES THE BRUINS' NEW COACH. Joe Juneau establishes team records for most assists by a rookie, with 70, and most points, with 102. Gordie Roberts becomes the first American-born player to play in 1,000 games. The Bruins win eight straight road games to tie a team record. Cam Neely's injury limits him to 13 games. The B's finish the season with eight straight wins en route to the Adams Division title, but are swept aside by Buffalo in the first round of the playoffs.

1993–94 CAN NEELY IS LIMITED TO 49 GAMES but scores 50 goals in his first 44. He wins the Masterson Trophy. Ray Bourque plays in his 1,100th game and wins his fifth Norris Trophy. Joe Juneau is traded to Washington for Al Iafrate. The Bruins finish the season at 42–29–13, good enough for second place behind Pittsburgh in the new Northeast Division. The B's beat the Canadiens in seven games in the first round of the play-offs but are ousted by the Devils in round two.

1994–95 AL IAFRATE MISSES THE ENTIRE SEASON with injuries. Cam Neely scores a league-leading 16 power-play goals. Adam Oates leads the team in scoring. The Bruins lead the league in penalty killing with an 86.9 percent success rate. The B's lose to the Devils in the conference quarterfinals.

1995–96 THE FLEETCENTER OPENS. CAM NEELY LEADS the Bruins in goals with 26. Al Iafrate misses his second straight season. The Bruins use five different goaltenders during the season. Kevin Stevens joins the club in a deal that sends Glen Murray and Bryan Smolinski to Pittsburgh. A disappointment, Stevens is sent on to Los Angeles for Rick Tocchet. The Bruins reach the playoffs for a record 29th year in a row but lose to the Florida Panthers in the opening round.

1996–97 RAY BOURQUE BECOMES THE BRUINS' ALL-TIME LEADING POINT SCORER. Adam Oates has a 20-game point-scoring streak. Using six goaltenders, the Bruins give up more than 300 goals. Play-by-play announcer Fred Cusick retires after 45 years. On March 1, the B's send Adam Oates and Bill Ranford to Washington in return for Jason Allison, Anson Carter, Jim Carey, and two draft choices. The Bruins finish with a losing record and miss the playoffs for the first time since 1966–67.

1997–98 PAT BURNS REPLACES STEVE KASPER behind the Boston bench. The Bruins acquire Dmitri Khristich and Byron Dafoe from the Kings in exchange for Sandy Moger, Jozef Stumpel, and a draft pick. In his first full season, Allison compiles 83 points for the team scoring lead and ninth place overall. Joe Thornton struggles in his NHL debut but rookie Sergei Samsonov excels with 47 points. Samsonov wins the Calder Trophy. Burns wins the Jack Adams Award as coach of the year. In the first round of the playoffs, the B's lose to Washington in six games.

1998–99 HARRY SINDEN ENTERS HIS TENTH SEASON as club president and his 27th as general manager, and receives the Lester Patrick Award. Jason Allison, the most improved player in 1997–98, leads the Bruins in points with 76. Dmitri Khristich leads the team in goals with 29. Ray Bourque, with 10 goals, ties Paul Coffey for the career goal-scoring lead among defensemen with 385. Pat Burns coaches his 750th NHL game on March 17. Goalie Byron Dafoe excels with a record of 32–23–11 and a 1.99 goals-against average. The Bruins qualify for the playoffs for the second consecutive year, with a mark of 37–28–17 for 91 points. They eliminate Carolina in the first round, but fall to Buffalo in the second round.

Bruins in the Hall of Fame

Name	Year Elected	With Bruins
Charles F. Adams	1960	1924–1936
Weston W. Adams	1972	1936–51, 1964–69
Marty Barry	1965	1929–1935
Leo Boivin	1986	1954–1966
Frank Brimsek	1966	1938–1949
Walter A. Brown	1962	1951–1964
John Bucyk	1981	1957–1978
Billy Burch	1974	1932–1933
Gerry Cheevers	1985	1965–72, 1975–80
Aubrey "Dit" Clapper	1947	1927–1947
Sprague Cleghorn	1958	1925–1928
Bill Cowley	1968	1935–1947
Cy Denneny	1959	1928–1929
Woody Dumart	1992	1935–42, 1945–54
Phil Esposito	1984	1967–1976
Ferny Flaman	1990	1945–52, 1954–56
Frank Frederickson	1958	1926–1929
Harvey Jackson	1971	1941–1944
Tom Johnson	1970	1963–1965
Guy Lapointe	1993	1983–1984
Harry Lumley	1980	1957–1960
Mickey MacKay	1952	1928–1930
Sylvio Mantha	1960	1936–1937
Harry Oliver	1967	1926–1934
Bobby Orr	1979	1966–1976
Bernie Parent	1984	1965–1967
Brad Park	1988	1975–1983
Jacques Plante	1978	1972–1973
Walter "Babe" Pratt	1966	1946–1947

Bill Quackenbush	1976	1949–1956
Jean Ratelle	1985	1975–1981
Arthur H. Ross	1945	1924–1954
Terry Sawchuk	1971	1955–1957
Milt Schmidt	1961	1936–42, 1946–55
Eddie Shore	1945	1926–1940
Albert "Babe" Siebert	1964	1933–1936
Harry Sinden	1983	1966–present
Reginald "Hooley" Smith	1972	1936–1937
Allan Stanley	1981	1956–1958
Nels Stewart	1962	1932–35, 1936–37
Cecil "Tiny" Thompson	1959	1928–1939
Ralph "Cooney" Weiland	1971	1928–1939